GOLD MAN
REVIEW

Gold Man Review is published once a year by Gold Man Publishing.

The editors invite submissions of previously unpublished works of fiction, nonfiction, and poetry. Manuscripts can be submitted at www.goldmanpublishing.com by following our submission guidelines.

Copyright 2018/2019 Gold Man Publishing / Gold Man Review LLC.
4626 Nantucket Drive
Redding, CA 96001
ISBN: 978-0-9969239-3-4

Address all requests to:
Heather Cuthbertson
Editor-in-Chief
Heather.Cuthbertson@GoldManPublishing.com

Contents

Issue 8 Editors Letter

Eight years.

Eight years.

I have to let that sink in.

When I first started Gold Man I couldn't see that number, couldn't see half that number. Not that I didn't think it was possible, but it was too far down the road. I guess time does fly by when you're having fun. In those years, I completed my MFA, got married, had three kids (one just last January), moved to California, bought a house, bought another house, wrote some novels, and taught when I could. Certainly, I've gained a lot, but I've lost some too. The biggest was losing both my parents within three months of each other in 2016. They left this Earth practically riding the same bus. You'd think they had one of those love stories that went back to grade school. The irony was they hated each other.

This year, I almost had another devastating loss in a way I never saw coming. This time it was my house. Last July it was directly in the path of the Carr Fire. I don't even know why it's still here. When I drive up the street to take my daughters to school, there's a burn path on a hill to the right where the fire had been eating its way toward my neighborhood.

It's easy to say it's just stuff. I told myself the same thing when I had left my house with just the clothes I was wearing and some of my mother's jewelry. It's all replaceable. But as I got on I-5 North and I could see flames descending in the direction of my house in West Redding, I ticked off all the things I left behind in my rush. The last blanket my mom bought for my kids. The program from my oldest daughter's first Christmas recital. My first publication. Countless little things that—even if I had time to prepare—would have been impractical to take as a wall of fire made its way toward us. But all those little things had added up to become part of my identity. Believing I was going back to ashes, it felt like I had been stripped of who I was.

The week I was evacuated was a nightmare. The whole time my mind cycled around one question: Is my house there? Is it there? *Is it there?????* In the end, I was one of the lucky ones because I had a home to return to when it was over. I'd taken my home for granted and you have no idea how much gratitude I felt that first moment I pulled into my driveway.

But there were so many who weren't so lucky.

For all the individuals and families who have lost their homes because of the fires that have been ravaging the West Coast, and to the families who lost everything in the Kilauea Volcano eruption, I understand that punch-in-the-gut sensation. That overwhelming feeling of loss. I know it wasn't just stuff. It was so much more.

We are the West Coast and we are a West Coast journal. We're here for you.

Sincerely,

Heather Cuthbertson
Editor-in-Chief

Gold Man Review Editors

Heather Cuthbertson
Editor-in-Chief

Darren Howard
Managing Editor

Marilyn Ebbs
Executive Editor

Nicklas Roetto
Project Editor

Daniel Link
Editor

Courtney Grela
Editor

With Special Thanks to Ashley Rich

poem

2018 Go-Going
chris menezes

A self

pushed Adderall
  to add to me
    to add to the economy

so I could get by
   or keep up
      and make enough
   and do enough
    without ever feeling
      like its enough

    Who holds the whip today?
    An Uncle Sam specter with blood-shot eyeballs?

    Who set the bar?
    Does it still glisten gold, or
    does it glow with what we're told its worth
    like numbers on a desktop
    backed-up by a plugged wall socket?

Amphetamines is a 15 billion dollar industry
   it made the 60's go-go
      experimenting with free
        dum, dum, dum

poor hippies with their poor
love, poor
communists, poor
socialists, poor
Cesar Chavez, poor
Dolores Huerta, poor
King, poor
dreams.

There's a big hot sun beating down
and we can't afford to slow down

4

Swordfishkebab

ron riekki

My strangest call ever was a man in a mom-and-pop grocery shop in L.A. who was impaled by a swordfish.

The guy was perfectly coherent. But wouldn't tell us anything.

Sir, can you hear me?

Sir, if you talk to us we'll know you have an airway. You'll make us worry less.

Sir, can you at least nod?

He nodded.

It was a big swordfish too.

The swordfish kind of nodded when the man nodded.

It was located in his LUQ.

Left upper quadrant.

That's where your stomach is.

Imagine eating swordfish all your life. You'd never think it would come through that way. Straight into the stomach. No trachea. No oropharynx. Just straight through the dermis. Just like a sword would.

You also have pancreas there. Kidney. Adrenal gland. Which I'm sure has sent him a shot of epinephrine. Because he's not feeling anything. Except that adrenaline high. But he looks calm. Strangely, he looks dopamined up. That's good old psychogenic shock.

But all those organs don't matter. What matters is the liver's there. The spleen. Highly vascular. The amount of hemorrhaging possible is massive.

Except he's got a giant plug inserted in him. And that plug is the swordfish. If we pull it out, he's going to arterial spurt like a full-cranked sprinkler system.

We're going to leave the swordfish in place. Wisely. And then, somehow, transport him to the hospital.

The guy's holding the swordfish, almost cradling it.

My partner goes out to get the stretcher. It's not something you're supposed to get by yourself, but we've been doing this a while now. It bangs on the equipment, but this is east side L.A. The equipment is from the 1800s. You can't break something that's already broken. There's absolutely no professionalism to its look. But the patients we see, they have other things to worry about than rust on a wheel.

My partner comes back in. No gurney.

He says he has shoulder pain.

So? I say.

No, it's just like, it doesn't feel right.

You want me to get it? I say.

He turns around, says he wants me to look, just in case.

I do. And his shirt is red. His white shirt has a red splotch. It's the reason our shirts are all white. So you can see pus yellow, purple venous bleeding, anything that lets you know you've just exposed yourself to something you didn't want to.

Did you catch it on something?

Why? What's back there? Is something back there?

Yeah, something's back there.

He reaches back, feels, retracts his hand, sees the blood.

What the?

Hold on, I say, and head to the door.

Wait, the guy on the floor says, don't go out there.

Why not?

The guy looks down at his stomach. This fish.

When we eat swordfish, they're usually only about three or four years old. We're eating toddlers. Pre-schoolers. Tasty infants.

And swordfish are ectothermic. They have special organs that heat their eyes. And those eyes are room temperature now. Looking straight down at a guy who's going to soon be in decompensated shock if we don't hurry.

I think he's shot, the guy says.

Me? my partner says.

He nods.

Why, what? Who shot me? What, you?

Of course he didn't shoot him. He hasn't done anything but lie there. Fish-trapped. And this fish, I've heard, can have almost fifty parasites inside it.

You do EMS near the ocean, you start learning about fish.

I've had two shark bite calls. Fish hooks in eyes. That's happened three times. Well, once in the eye. The two other times, it was different parts of the face. A guy who choked to death swallowing live goldfish. About a billion jellyfish stings. I could keep going.

Who shot me? my partner shouts.

They did.

I look at my partner and before I can say it, he says, A.R.

Additional resources.

That means 911.

That means get the cops here.

He pulls out his phone.

The guy on the floor rubs his face, says, You might want to get away from the windows.

We do. We back up as far as we can. We can't get anything out of the ambulance now. We don't have our MedPacks. A huge error. Those are supposed to go in for every call, but this was an Unknown Medical. So many calls are Unknown Medical. I guess it's hard to describe something like this. Instead they call in, say, Ummm, I think you want to send someone here. Our Med-Packs are safe and cozy in the back of the ambulance, where they're useless.

Did it feel like you got shot? I ask.

No, he says.

What did it feel like?

Nothing. Just, I opened the door and my shoulder just—

He doesn't finish the sentence.

911 has answered. He tells them what's going on, gives the address, says he's not sure, but thinks there's a gunman out there somewhere. They say to hold on, a unit's on the way.

We wait. Backing up as far as we can. Back wall.

And then someone walks in the front door. A man with a politician's face. A man with clothes that scream white-collar. A haircut like he wishes he was a French cinematographer.

He sees the guy on the floor. The swordfish. Sees us.

Store's closed, my partner says.

The guy spins around, pep in his step, as if he's just seen something cool, and leaves.

Listen, my partner says.

We do.

We're waiting for the sound of a gunshot.

Of someone in pain.

There's just the dull sounds of L.A.

The city can be so quiet even with four million people.

I bend over, take the swordfish guy's pulse.

What's your name?

The cops are coming? he says.

My partner laughs, once. No comedy to it.

I finish counting. He's about one hundred, I say.

That's it? my partner asks.

Is that good? the guy asks.

Sixty to a hundred is normal, I say. For pulse.

So I'm normal, he says.

You're lying down, not moving, I say, you'd expect to be on the lower end. You're on the higher end. It's borderline tachycardia.

Is that good? he asks.

Is there a back door to this place? I ask.

We're not going anywhere, my partner says.

I should probably tell you who he is, my partner. Fred Rypponen. Finn-ish. The only Finnish guy in Los Angeles. He's dating a Russian ob/gyn nurse and a Brazilian radiology technician at the same time. Neither of them know it. He says this way he doesn't care if one of them leaves him. He's a func-tioning alcoholic. An athletic 25-year-old who in ten years will probably be bald, bedridden, or dead. He's on his way there now.

I stand up, grab my partner's wrist.

I can do it myself, he says.

I don't listen to him. I count.

One-twenty, I say.

No.

Yeah, you're basically running full speed right now. You might want to sit down, I say.

He sits, takes his own pulse.

I stand there. Silent.

My partner knows what I'm doing.

I'm counting breaths. Silence is perfect for respiratory status. You can't tell how fast someone's breathing when they're talking.

Swordfish guy is around twenty-two breaths. My partner's around sixteen, but that's because he was controlling his breath because he knew I was counting. He wanted it to be perfectly average. The more someone understands medicine, the tougher of a patient they are. The worst patient of all is the heroin addict. They know medicine like Harvard Med doctoral students. They have to. It's their job. You can only get painkillers if you know how to fake all of the symptoms of someone who needs painkillers.

What I love about a patient like this, a patient with a fish stabbed through his gut, is that you can't lie. You can't pretend to be impaled by a swordfish. There's nothing hypochondriac about it. It's just good, true, honest medicine.

That we can't practice.

Why?

The b.p.'s in the thing, I say.

What's that? the guy on the floor asks.

The sphygmomanometer, I say, trying to pronounce it correctly, but failing.

What's that? the guy on the floor asks.

He's got a lot of questions.

We got questions too. What's your name? Why is a goddamn swordfish in your spleen? And who the hell shot me? my partner says.

I'm sorry about that, he says.

Take your shirt off, I say to Fred.

Juggling two patients is hell. I'm forgetting everything right now. All of the basic BLS skills. They always told us in EMT school not to get hurt on the job, that if you do, your partner suddenly has to work alone on double the patients. That's me.

No, Fred says.

Don't make me get you trauma naked, I say.

Fred takes off his shirt. Flexes. He can't help not. He's one of those guys at the gym that's a mirror addict. Something very much psychologically wrong about those types. He's torturing his heart with excess weightlifting followed by excess drinking followed by more excess weightlifting followed by more excessive drinking. The types who get heart attacks in their late thirties and can't figure out why.

You know, the guy on the floor says, you both might want to get behind this counter.

I try to find the bullet hole on his back. There isn't one. I tell him this.

Keep looking, he says, you know.

'You know' means that bullet holes are easily missed. The blood covers them. The holes are small. Going in. Going out they're big. But I don't see either.

You sure you were shot? I ask. And then I see it. The littlest thing. The cutest little hole. The nicest little gurgling.

Here, I say.

You got it?

I nod.

Son of a bitch, he says. Son of a bitch. Shot. Dammit. No way. Damnit.

It's fine, I say.

Yeah, sure, fine, he says, perfect.

It's upper, clavicle, I don't know, maybe nicked bone.

But it's bleeding?

Yeah.

Like occlusive dressing bleeding?

No, like in the future it'll be cool to tell people you've been shot. Just sit down. Relax. Keep your heart rate low. Keep sitting up, I say, you'll live.

You'll live, he says, making a fist.

We both look at the floor.

Are you going to do anything for me? the swordfish guy says.

We don't even know who you are, my partner says.

What does that have to do with anything?

There's nothing we can do, I say. You got an airway.

What's that mean?

You're talking. You're speaking. You're breathing. You're not bleeding. Much, I mean.

Is it in my heart? he asks.

My partner does his solitary laugh again. No, it's not in your heart. If it was in your heart, you'd be dead, my partner says.

The grocery store is tiny for L.A. It's got poverty written into its floors. Kleenex everywhere. Books on the floor. Racquetballs, which don't seem for sale, just tossed around inexplicably. And, everywhere, canned food—stacked, tumbled, on their sides, upside-down, dented, boxed, open, closed.

I see a cop car drive by.

No siren.

No speeding.

Just going right by. And gone.

Was that our guy? my partner asks.

I shrug.

Did you tell them you were shot?

Yeah, maybe I shouldn't have. They hate EMS.

This is Wednesday. My second shift of the week. I'm a part-timer. No medical benefits. Shit pay. A roll of the dice that I'd get this call. And something about it I'm fine with. I don't mind it. Maybe it's that I'm getting paid not to work. Maybe it's knowing that I can brag now that I had a partner get shot on shift. Maybe it's that I served during Desert Storm, so this isn't really a big deal. It's just L.A. It's normal.

Are they going to come in here? I ask, whoever shot him?

The guy on the floor nods no.

Did you get messed up with the Mafia or something?
He nods no.
Or gang members or something?
Or something, he says.
My partner chimes in, Can you just let us know what's going on? We'll tell the cops you were helpful to us.
Do you have any water? he says.
My partner nods no.
The guy points behind Fred. A cooler filled with bottles.
Pick any, the guy says.
Fred reaches in, grabs one.
A Vitamin Water, the guy says.
Fred puts the bottle back, takes out a Vitamin Water.
We realize he's been holding the swordfish in place the whole time. Can't move his hands. Must be exhausted.
Can we get chairs and prop this or something? I ask.
We can't.
There aren't any chairs.
Put him on his side? my partner offers up.
We can't.
I hold the swordfish. My partner gives him the Vitamin Water.
He drinks.
Those are crap for you, my partner says, rot your teeth.
Already are, he says.
And he's right. His teeth look like deep vein thrombosis. They look like fetal alcohol syndrome. They look like they have cancer. If there was such a thing as teeth cancer.
He drinks again, sloppy. Choking. Coughing.
Careful, my partner says.
He drinks again. Finishes the whole bottle.
The fish is slippery. Heavy. I have to work at keeping it in place. Knowing that if it moves around, it'll cause damage, widen the hole, perhaps kick in a vagal response, shut down his heart rate, tear an artery, a whole list of medical problems going through my imagination. I don't know. This is beyond my training. Beyond my scope of practice.
Is this thing all the way through your back? I ask.
I don't know, he says.
Are you stuck to the floor?
I don't know, he says.
What's it called anyway, I ask.
A beak? my partner says.
A fin. No, not a fin.
I'm a Finn, my partner says.
He's Finnish, I explain.
If this was any city anywhere else in the world, the cops would be here by now, my partner says.
Call again, I say.

He doesn't. He reaches into the cooler, looks to the guy on the floor, to see if it's OK.

Go ahead, he says.

We see a police car pull up in front of the store, a cop getting out. No concern. Calm. Bored. He ambles his way to the door.

My partner gets a water, drinks.

$2.75, the guy says.

That much? my partner says.

Yes.

He drinks again.

$2.75, he repeats.

Yeah?

He wants you to pay, I say.

Fred puts the bottle down. Doesn't know what to say.

It's how I live, the guy says.

poem

Wormwood

myrlin a. hermes

Your absence is an odd shape.
Nothing else fits into it.

Twisty little hole,

I am riddled.

Unspecified Relation

stephanie barbé hammer

Should I start off by telling you that Carter Bergman shot himself right before he graduated from Columbia Law School two and a half years ago or is that jumping the gun narratively speaking?

Yeah. But he'd like it. He had a dark sense of humor.

Should I remind you how hard it is to get into Columbia Law?

Who was Carter Bergman to me anyway?

Here is what he was not:

- my age.
- my son.
- my lover.
- my student.
- (my) drug dealer.

He was an unspecified relation. An almost adopted somebody.

Let's talk about why I was mad at him and why he bought me two orange plastic toy guns as an apology.

I'd sent a bunch of gifts to Carter his freshman year at NYU. That was ten years ago. I remember a subscription to the *Wall Street Journal* and I remember in particular some gleaming stack of silver snack tins from Dean and Deluca. I sent some to my daughter and then sent some to him. He enjoyed luxurious things like that because he was a former New Yorker, as am I. He went to an exclusive private boys' school in Manhattan.

The first boy to ever kiss me went to that school.

Now, that's an admittedly weird somewhat Oedipal connection because perhaps Carter could be the son of that boy. Making Carter quite literally the son I never had.

Anyway, Carter never wrote me a thank you note, or email, or in any way expressed appreciation for these gifts.

I'm pissed off right now just thinking about it.

So how did I get the guns?

Chanukah, nine years ago. Here's what happens.

Carter turns up at our house in lower Beverly Hills with this huge wrapped package containing two bright orange plastic toy guns. One is a rifle and one is a six-shooter. They have brown handles that have been decorated with those curlicues to look like cowboy guns.

A child's present—from one NYC kid to another.

The rifle got broken in our move from the Beverly Hills house to greater Los Angeles, but the six-shooter remains intact.

Should I tell you that the orange plastic gun travels with me and sits in the middle kitchen drawer for creative inspiration? It's gone up and down the

West Coast and beyond.

I used it in my first novel. The hero plays with this orange toy gun when he is pretending to be a cowboy. He shoots it at Mr. Death, his enemy.

Is now the time to explain how I got to know Carter in the first place? Here's what happens.

My daughter brings home this boy home from school one day. He has transferred to her high school. His mother has killed herself. Or she has OD'd. The details are tragic but unclear.

He sits in our small but tastefully decorated living room in Beverly Hills. To quote my mother, he entertains us with his wit and charm.

Is now the time to admit that I can't reproduce how Carter talked or what he said exactly because he said it so fast you had to listen with all your attention just to follow the acrobatics of his argumentation and observation?

He was what they call wicked smart.

Carter and my kid became best friends for the rest of high school. Recently, she discovered a yearbook photo of the two of them arguing and gesticulating.

How did I come to feel so attached to this friend of my daughter's? This is how.

Senior year of high school, Carter wins a fiction-writing prize. He invites me to the celebration at the high school. I put on my new makeup and my new expensive raincoat because—as always—I want to look good for my daughter. When I get to the school, I realize that I am the only non-high-school official adult present to share in Carter's triumph. I have become a kind of family stand-in.

Should I say that I feel bad that his mother isn't there, but that I also feel honored and special?

Should I admit that I feel—rightly or wrongly—chosen?

I don't remember the piece he read. It was a quasi-comical horrid adaptation of something classical … *The Iliad? Oedipus Rex?* I can't call it forth. It was funny. We all laughed. I think he was stoned at the party. His eyes seemed glazed.

"Drugs," my mother said to me on more than one occasion. "Drugs put you out of control and make you do and say things you'd never do or say otherwise."

Is it time to tell you that there was something really wrong with my mother? Trauma, or borderline personality, or extreme narcissism, or social anxiety? Is it time to tell you that she rarely hugged me or even touched me? That she was terrified of the telephone and of all appliances and machines?

That she feared and detested most people?

Do you feel sorry for her?

I want to. Sometimes I manage it.

This kind of parenting messes up a person.

Is now the time to mention that Carter was not always a nice person and that I was not a nice person about it?

Here's what happens.

A year or so after the gun gift, Carter behaves cruelly to my daughter. I don't see this cruelty occurring. I am busy cutting bagels or pouring wine and talking to guests at our annual un-Xmas party that we used to have for all the Jews and Buddhists and atheists who didn't exactly celebrate Xmas, but who had no place to go.

But, apparently, he makes some really nasty, sarcastic comments to her that are so bad she runs out of the house and hides in the alley until after he leaves.

Should I tell you that I found out about this incident only after the party was over? That I didn't even notice that my daughter wasn't at the party?

What kind of mother does that? What kind of mother is that wrapped up in cutting bagels and talking to guests that she doesn't notice that her kid is AWOL?

Perhaps it's the kind of mother who says, "What do you need dinner for?" at a cocktail party when you are six and she is busy entertaining the guests.

You complain.

She hands you a couple of olives.

That kind.

After the Un-Xmas party incident, my husband told me I could not have Carter over to the house. My daughter stopped speaking to him altogether.

But should I tell you that I felt badly?

But I didn't feel badly enough.

Because, when Carter came back into town, I would semi-sneak out of the house and go and meet him for coffee or lunch and not tell anyone what I was doing and hope I didn't run into anyone I knew who would rat on me to my family.

So … is now the time to mention that Carter was a drug dealer? Which is perhaps why he owned the gun that he shot himself with?

Do you hate him a lot yet?

Do you hate me for putting up with him?

Or worse—for finding him so *interesting?*

Is now the time to mention that the writer in me was curious about Carter's drug-dealing life? The writer part was curiouser than the parental part of me that should have been concerned about this young person doing something illegal and dangerous.

Is now the time to tell you that I went over to Carter's house once and he demonstrated how to send drugs through the mail? And that I used that information subsequently in my novel?

Let me tell you about Carter's house.

This may be all wrong but it's what I remember.

In my mind's eye is a big house on an exclusive block in Beverly Hills, but the inside is a combination of Miss Havisham's and my grandparents' Russian aristocrats-in-exile-catastrophe house in New York City. As I remember it—and I think I've already established that I'm not so reliable—it's filled with dusty expensive French furniture, pictures that were standing against the wall and not hung up, scratches and holes in the paint, and the air smells stale, like no one ever opened the windows. I don't see anyone there but

Carter's nanny, who is smoking. I remember that he bums a cigarette off her. The two of them don't talk much, but—and this is going to sound stupid—I feel the love between them. As though this whole place is a wreck but these two people—they care about each other.

Then we go upstairs.

Is now the time to mention that Carter shows me all his mother's coats? They are hanging in his closet. This does not freak me out because I think my daughter has already told me about it—how he has kept all her things.

Should I mention that—when I see those coats—a part of me is jealously hopeful?

Should I admit that when I look in the closet I think I "I hope my daughter is so broken up when I die that she keeps all my coats?"

Is now the time to mention that when I was a teenager I wore my mother's vintage clothes? It was a way to inhabit her skin. A way to be close to her. It grieved me that I looked nothing like her. I was always so far away from her.

Should I mention that my kid looks nothing like me at all? She looks a bit like Carter. They are both blondes with blue eyes.

Is now the time to mention that Carter shot himself right before he was supposed to attend my book launch in NYC?

Yes, it IS all about me.

I had been in touch with Carter on Facebook about the book launch and I'd invited him. But I didn't phone him to talk about plans. Because if I did, I was going to have to tell him something like:

• I feel disloyal to my daughter being connected to you when she won't even talk to you.

• You need to apologize to her.

So, I put off calling him. And the night before I was going to fly to New York, my daughter telephoned me to tell me that Carter was dead.

"You better sit down," she said. Which was a thoughtful thing to say.

Is now the time to speculate as to why Carter killed himself? There are several possibilities:

• He was bi-polar

• He was addicted

• He was discouraged because he didn't have a great job lined up and when you go to Columbia that's what you're supposed to have

• He was unable to fulfill his dream of becoming a writer

• He couldn't stand not being the smartest person in the room anymore (my daughter's theory)

• Something else altogether

He left a long suicide note. I have not seen it.

Now perhaps might be the time to mention the last in-person conversation I had with Carter. Here's what happens.

We sit in *Pain Quotidien* near the therapists' and plastic surgeons' offices in Beverly Hills. He tells me an absolutely hilarious story about his failed summer internship interviews. He enacts his approach with said Park Avenue law firms and shows me how he did his LEVEL BEST TO ACT LIKE A

TEAM PLAYER AND A GOOD CORPORATE CAPITALIST. And he does an impression of himself looking fascinated by these firms' books of business and political connections.

I laugh till I cry. We eat extra croissants and drink extra coffee during that visit, which goes on for hours because there's so much to say and so much to hear and so much to share.

Should I share that I was proud of Carter for not getting a job like that? But shouldn't I have showed a bit more *concern?*

Now, all I have left is a voicemail message from him in November and a few Facebook messages.

And the orange toy gun.

Is now the time to mention that since I couldn't cancel my trip to New York, I said Kaddish for Carter on the corner of 77th Street and Madison Avenue (which is a very fancy, exclusive block), while his funeral was going on in Los Angeles?

I stand, and recite the prayer using my smartphone. Then I cry. Then I go shopping. Then I go to the *Pain Quotidien* near my grandparents' house.

I come back to Los Angeles and I write about him. I write poems and I write stories. He's still dead.

I pick out a burial plot for me and my husband in the Jewish cemetery in Los Angeles where Carter and his mother are.

Is now the moment to mention that I keep on wondering what will happen to Carter's mother's coats?

My mother did not wish to be buried. Her ashes were scattered in Southampton New York on the beach.

My daughter says she also wants to be cremated.

Are the words I am writing lethal or salutary?

How crappy a mother am I?

How crappy a daughter was I?

Same answer. Crappy. I was not and am not a particularly easy person to deal with. Take my obsession with presents, for example. And why can't I just forgive my mother? She was really messed up, obviously. What the hell is wrong with me that I can't let go of all this?

In closing, should I talk about that one-time Carter made me drive him to his grandparents' house in LA?

For the record, I HATE TO DRIVE. But yes, I did it. I remember thinking, "God damn it," at the same time as I wanted to help him.

Is now the time to tell you that my mother couldn't drive? Couldn't even learn?

I guess that's something—isn't it?

In this memory, Carter slides into the passenger seat and says, "I want to tell you something," and in this memory, I'm hating to navigate all that insane Los Angeles traffic and talk to him and listen to him at the same time.

But still I say to Carter, "Shoot."

A True Gift

linda ferguson

Just as I was about to give my speech the lights went off, so I stood there in the dark auditorium and quickly came up with a witty line to say when the power came back on.

And let there be light—that was what I'd say.

I could already feel the warmth of my audience's response, my approval ratings skyrocketing. Standing on the brink of such success was like basking in the golden rays of an October afternoon.

Beautiful.

But when the lights did come on again, I was so surprised I forgot all about my clever line and stared dumbfounded at my audience because—prepare yourself, this was odd—every one of them was now wearing a wig.

This was not the case before the snafu with the power. Then, there were the usual array of hairdos—the balding heads, the braids and buns, the mohawks, the faux hawks, the perms, the buzz cuts, the glowing Jesus locks—etcetera, etcetera.

Now all of those were suddenly gone and replaced with wigs in one of two styles: blond spun-sugar strands and a black cap of hair, as polished as river rock.

The long blond strands were sticky (unfortunate flies that landed there would never launch again) and molded in perpetual motion—a windswept sculpture perched on people's heads.

It was something.

And then there were the people in the other wig, which clutched the scalp at the temples and was so dark and shiny I thought I caught a whiff of black licorice.

Standing there with my own hair tucked behind my ears, I felt out of place and wished I'd worn the wig I'd inherited from my grandmother, the cropped russet curls clipped back with an emerald bobby pin. But there was no time to linger over this regret because I still had a presentation to give.

I was an experienced speaker and although the wig business was strange, I was ready to roll with it. So, I plunged right into my speech, only to send the evening lurching completely off the rails. Instead of saying the words I'd practiced, I was talking in a language I didn't know, speaking in neither Spanish nor Gaelic nor Vietnamese. This was not Icelandic or Quechua or Swahili; each word was completely unrecognizable—at least, that is, to me.

Yet somehow, I was saying *something*, speaking some specific language that was clearly comprehensible to the wig people, the spun-sugar and the licorice, all of whom were united in their response.

Picture my winged popularity pierced by an arrow and plunging with rapidity.

You could say my wig-wearing audience was displeased, agitated, riled up, enraged. I saw visible signs of this: lips pinched, temples pulsed, knuckles ground into palms—a mortar and pestle effect—and I concluded that the speech I was delivering against my will was not the one I had down, the one I'd rehearsed so many times it rolled off my tongue with the ease of rhyming couplets.

That one would have had the wearer of each wig gleaming with appreciation, but this speech I was giving was an irritant.

Times ten.

Times ten million.

Faces turned red, and what began as grumbling quickly developed into a galloping herd of iron-clad hooves—metaphorically speaking—just as an overripe tomato—literally—arced through the heated air and landed—*splat!*—on my left shoulder like an epaulet.

This isn't happening, I thought and tried speaking again, but each new syllable I uttered added another splash of gasoline onto a pyre that was already devouring the oxygen in the room faster than a dragon's breath.

One hothead in a licorice wig even threw a *can* of tomatoes at me. Luckily, I had quick reflexes and was able to duck in time. The can hit the wall behind me then bounced back and rolled off the stage before I could grab it. Disappointing, certainly, because I had a recipe for a ratatouille that called for canned tomatoes, and now if I wanted to make it, I'd have to stop at the store on my way home, but *no matter*, I told myself, as people rose from their seats, fists raised.

One gripped a pitchfork, and another looped the end of a rope.

It was clearly time to scoot, so I opened my mouth to briefly thank everyone for coming and almost laughed when I heard the sound I was issuing now: Aaaaaah.

This elongated utterance reverberated to me from the stage speakers, and, quite oddly, seemed to soothe my roiling audience like a sedative that took instant effect. Lips softened, fists opened and wigs that had gone askew in the tumult I'd unwittingly created seemed to straighten of their own accord. I took a chance and opened my mouth again and spoke:

Aaaaaah, I said, and—get this—a soft aaaaah murmured back from somewhere in the center of the room. Then another one, deeper—a baritone—came from the front rows.

Talk about making lemonade.

My unfortunate situation had morphed into an opportunity to realize my lifelong secret and cherished dream of conducting a choir or a symphony.

Aaaaah, I said, raising my hands, inviting more audience members to join in, and as a wave of aaaaah's rolled back, I glowed like a kindergartner who'd just earned her first gold star.

It was a dance—a call and response. Walls, floor, and ceiling gently bouncing the pleasing sound around like an iridescent bubble in the breeze. You felt it on your skin like a warm bath. Tensed shoulders nestled back into their sockets while heartrates softened into pastel sighs.

Seizing the moment, I motioned to the those sitting on the right side of the room to begin aaahing, and then motioned to those on the left, then scooped my hands to indicate I wanted to hear them aaah all together, and they did, just as I directed.

Over the crowd, a pleasant ease descended. Some sank low in their seats and yawned. Children snuggled into their parent's laps. Others rested their heads on their neighbor's shoulders, and their neighbor's arms circled round them amidst a breath of aaaaah's, and the room was now peaceful as a blue blanket.

Eyelids fell like snow.

And all because of my speech.

This was better than anything I could have planned, I thought as I tiptoed out the door, leaving my audience to enjoy their little rest.

Outside, I saw a train in the distance, but I was still floating on the sweet cloud of my unexpected success. I decided to walk home despite all the forest fires that had been blazing outside of the city lately and the smoke that instantly irritated my throat.

The moon was full and orange-red, a bold twin of the setting sun—the air as silent as the looming smoke—no car alarm, or ringtone or train horn.

Thinking, suddenly, of the raging emotions I'd somehow sparked earlier in my audience, I shivered. But, I told myself, there was nothing I could do about that now so there was no point in lingering on that thought.

Thanks to my new air conditioning, I'd been able to have the windows to my house closed the entire week, which kept out all but a trace of smoke, and I was looking forward to opening a book and a bottle of wine and spending a cozy evening at home. The perfect way to relish yet another personal triumph.

The Kodiak Brown Bear

tanyo ravicz

I was with two others one evening on Kodiak Island when a mother brown bear charged us in defense of her cubs. We had unintentionally surprised her in the spruce forest in the twilight, and she reacted instinctively and charged to ten feet of us. We responded by climbing onto the roof of a derelict cabin and staying there. Maybe later, we'd be able to say what we meant to do with the rusty axes we took with us. I could spin an ax through the air and sink it into the side of a spruce tree twenty feet away, a trick I had learned from some Athabaskan Indians, but I wasn't about to try my axmanship against an angry brown bear.

The bear woofed at us in warning and bawled at her cubs to climb down from the spruce tree into which they had fled. This "woofing" of a brown bear is a violent exhalation of air from its lungs, repeated and interspersed with growls. The bear stood on her back feet and raked her claws through the tree bark, looking up at her cubs, and they eventually descended and went away with her.

Bears woof and huff and gnash their teeth when agitated, and I was fine with waiting on the cabin roof for as long as this bear needed to get her woof out. I remembered a case in interior Alaska of a black bear that pursued a woman onto a cabin roof and killed her. We don't have black bears on Kodiak Island, but forgive me for not putting all my trust in the notion that adult brown bears won't climb. It reminds me of my Canadian friend who, when I had moved to Alaska, mischievously advised me, "Just remember, bears can't run downhill."

Sooner or later every resident of rural Kodiak crosses paths with a brown bear. Their paths will cross more than once. I was hiking the mountain south of Cottonwood, my wilderness homestead on Kodiak Island's north coast, when I met a brown bear with a white blaze on his back, a four-pointed star in the rich dark fur. I quit the area at once. The next morning, I avoided the mountaintop and hiked the seashore, but the bear had the same idea. There he was at Eagle Rock, same white blaze on his back, standing upright and gazing seaward like a captain anxiously awaiting his next commission.

The taxonomy of the Kodiak brown bear has long been disputed. The Kodiak bear was once considered a separate species. Today the North American brown bear is said to include both the Kodiak bear and the mainland grizzly bear, but not all scientists agree that the Kodiak bear's bigger size and anatomical differences entitle it to its own subspecies (*Ursus arctos middendorffi*). Kodiak bears have been insulated here since the glaciers retreated at the end of the Pleistocene and it stands to reason they are genetically distinct. Kodiak has a subspecies of short-tailed weasel for the same reason: it lives only on the Kodiak Archipelago. The local Visitors' Guide for 2017 informs us, "The Kodiak bear is a subspecies of the brown or grizzly bear and is the largest bear in the world," a declaration that will keep the tribes of Linnaeus warring for another century—and will annoy the champions of the polar bear, who insist that the polar bear is bigger than the Kodiak brown bear. These battles often come down to competing word choices and standards of measurement. Kodiak Island, measured in miles of coastline, is the largest island in the United States, but measured in square miles it is second to Hawaii. Taxonomically, the Kodiak bear is a flesh-eating carnivore, but in practice the bear is an omnivore who enjoys grass and berries and fish.

It's safe to say, I hope, that the Kodiak bear is a brown bear who inhabits the Kodiak Archipelago. He is one of the largest living land carnivores on the planet—the male can easily weigh over half a ton—so it's wise to remember he's out there. A paradox of living with brown bears is that you want nothing to do with them, but it feels such a privilege to live among them. Without bears there wouldn't be the same air of wildness and consequence that hangs over the country, the same tautening of the senses that checks the dulling of habit, the same deep and real and fearsome context against which to joy in the finer pleasures of a wildflower or a bird's song. The special atmosphere of a place inhabited by these bears correlates, I suppose, with the overall scarceness of the bears, with their diminished numbers elsewhere, their virtual extermination from the vast range where they once flourished. Meriwether Lewis calls these bears, interchangeably, grizzlies and brown bears, "tremendous animals," he writes in his journal, whose ferocity could only be conquered "by a shot in the head." I am a bit brokenhearted when I read Lewis and Clark, not because I think them callous or cruel, it's because I know their heroism was inseparable from their ignorance, from how much they didn't understand.

In the past, drawn by the mystique of the brown bears, I fought down an impulse to follow them. This strange pull, this gravitation, was strongest in my early years at Cottonwood when I was alone at the homestead and more susceptible if not more reckless. I stood in forest twilight admiring the fluid grace of a brown bear padding soundlessly by, the loft of its head, the smoothly moving muscles of its hip and shoulder, and I longed to follow the bear and I sometimes followed a ways. Today when I see a brown bear, I act to avert a meeting, and I assume the same is true of the bears. They impress me with their size and majesty, in keeping with their mystique—"furious and formidable," Meriwether Lewis writes—but in truth a bear can be a base creature, a hunger-driven scavenger leading a dismal animal existence. The insects harass him and a raven's squawk startles him. For every anecdote of the bear's grandeur there's another that paints him a clown or petty criminal. A teenager bear broke into so-and-so's cabin and snatched a candy bar. A bear ate a bucketful of paint and a pipeful of Freon and when the owners came home they found him slumped across the open chest freezer.

It's hard to overstate the bears' influence on our lives at Cottonwood. Punctured tires, a torn inflatable boat, a ruined outhouse door—this partial list of the bear damage we've sustained over the years is the least of it. The bears became an everyday contingency like the weather. We heard their nasal bawling in the bush, we heard their doggish panting when they swept past our window, or a bear heard us first and startled us by standing in the vegetation to better see us. Our choices at Cottonwood have been guided by the bears in significant ways—the decision to build a solar electric fence—and innumerable small ways like which direction to hike on a given day. Every kind of brown bear is here, light brown and chocolate and golden in color, mature males, adolescents, females with cubs, the cool, standoffish bears of midsummer, the temperamental bears of autumn, bears by moonlight, bears in snow, bears on the mountain and bears down below.

Wherever I had lived in Alaska, in the populated environs of Fairbanks and Anchorage, wild bears lived nearby and they sometimes clashed with people. But to live in the Kodiak bush, to share a roadless wilderness with the bears, a country in which the bears outnumber the people—this felt different. It felt total. And I was immersed in this new world right away. To round a bend in the trail and encounter brown bears—it's unnerving. Five miles east of Cottonwood, at Port Bailey Cannery, a brown bear was shot after it reared up on a cannery worker. Martina and the children would eventually join me at Cottonwood and I became anxious about the risks. "There is nothing like a bear track to arouse the imagination," Adolph Murie writes, and how true it is. I had absurd nightmares of being chased by the bears. In one dream the bear yelled "To hell with equal rights!" before he bashed the door in and came after me.

A large male and several females with cubs ranged through Cottonwood, and my glimpses of them kept me on edge. A bear moves with natural grace but is careless who hears him, and only a bear in the bush, heavy and unafraid, sets off such a slow sustained snapping of branches. This was a sound I heard as I explored the country on foot or as I worked about the cabin, tilling the garden or painting the siding—

> A tramping in the woods that nobody
> but he could make alerted me, and I
> pricked up listening, all newborn with suspense
> to see where he'd emerge.
> I'd turned so quickly, apprehensive,
> disoriented, not knowing where he was,
> I was momentarily blinded by the sun
> high in the southwest sky.
> But when he came, it was at an amble,
> adolescent, just this side of frisky,
> from under the five or six big spruce trees,
> not knowing that the man
> who had dropped his paintbrush and backed away
> was just as startled as he. I repented,
> I laughed aloud and called him back by name,
> but, nameless, he didn't stay.

The most abundant bear sign, the commonest reminder of the bears' presence, is their droppings. "Bear sign" is an esoteric phrase that basically means crap. I must have been chasing a scout badge or entering a post-poetry poetry contest when I kept this catalog:

> fresh sign, black and shiny, between gully and section line
> enormous olive-colored grassy heap of bear scat
> green and lumpy like horse apples
> a gigantic pile of porridge
> oozy wet & black
> blue-black with berry seeds
> drying mounds of seaweed-laden excrement

A careful observation of bear droppings is no doubt essential practice for the Alaskan woodsman.

Bear sign includes, more broadly, tracks and other evidences of the bears' presence: the hollows in which they bed down, the branches they rip from a tree, the raked earth and torn moss, the stray tufts of their hair. Bears shed their fur when they roll on the ground or when they catch on a branch. They also have favorite rubbing trees where they stand and scratch their backs. One such tree is a thin whitish spruce free of spurs and heavily scored by bear claws. Clumps of auburn hair stick in the spruce sap and cling in the creases of the bark after the bear has gone. I whistled at a bear who was rubbing his back here and he looked over at me and squinted as if he couldn't believe anyone else knew the refrain from Tom T. Hall's "Old Dogs, Children and Watermelon Wine."

In the late 1990s brown bears were more active on the Kupreanof Peninsula than at any time in living memory. A reduced food supply after seasons of adverse weather, poor salmon returns, the climatic cycle known as El Niño—the peak bear activity was attributed to any and all of these phenomena. A staffer at the Kodiak National Wildlife Refuge speculated that the nature-pampered Kodiak brown bears would have to get their paws dirty and to scrounge for roots and grubs the way the grizzlies of interior Alaska always had to, and she warned me that the bears wouldn't go down easy for the winter, not before they ate enough food to store the fat and nutrients they needed to survive.

She was right. In the trying autumn of 1998, a season that extended into December, we saw or heard brown bears almost daily, and it put a strain on our family. At times, Martina didn't forgive me for the homestead. Kody was a year old and Miranda was six years old and we felt vulnerable. News of a mauling at Terror Bay reached us. The bears periodically ripped our tarps or ransacked a tote. They tracked the snow around the cabin. The delight we had experienced in September when a mother and triplets frolicked outside our window turned inexorably to jitters. I bought a cordless spotlight for the dark nights and I strung a tripwire alarm around our supply tent. It's no good for a cub to learn from its mother to poke around people's cabins and we took precautions to avoid this. We kept a clean cabin and removed all our food waste. During hikes we packed a bear horn and a shotgun. I always carried the shotgun, even in rain, and with my son on my back. "Coming through, bear, coming through!" To carry the gun and to dry and oil it every day was a chore, but I would not have forgiven myself for not having the gun as a fallback in an emergency. There is such a thing as a mean-tempered bear, a bear that in human terms is just plain mean, and while the mean bear is no doubt the exception, nobody who goes among wild bears should hold nature in so little esteem as to deny its exceptions. Willy Fulton, the pilot who in 2003 discovered the scant remains of bear researchers Timothy Treadwell and Amie Huguenard at Kaflia Bay, across Shelikof Strait from us, tells me that the bear that stalked him there and that made a meal of Treadwell and Huguenard was well known to be a mean-tempered bear.

Brown bears seldom attack people unless provoked, and the common-sense advice is don't provoke the bears, but in wild country, it's not possible to eliminate every potential misunderstanding. Bears are individuals with their own quirks and peeves. A foraging bear can be surprisingly oblivious, and no matter how careful you are, you may walk up on one. Bears have run from me; bears have ignored me; and most have behaved with calm discretion and moved on. The few bears that harassed us around the cabin were adolescent bears. I only once saw a bear that I instinctively felt was ill-natured and even vicious, one that turned on us with a malevolent scowl when it heard my family approaching on foot. To this day, the bear's expression chills me when I think of it. He was occupied with some object in the grass, I didn't see what, but the glower on his face, his disgruntlement, went beyond possessiveness, and I only knew it was essential that we withdraw.

There wasn't an uninhabited cabin in the miles around Cottonwood that wasn't hit by brown bears that autumn. Gaping doors, punched-out windows and ransacked interiors were the tell. We saw two bears at it in November, batting around the items they had dragged from a tiny hunting cabin—a cooler, a funnel, a plastic storage container. At another cabin we found broken glass and bloody paw prints. Even Alderwood Lodge was hit, a wilderness lodge four miles east of us. The doors of bungalows and outbuildings hung open. A window was shattered over the lodge entry. The bear had smashed the front doorknob and broken the lock. He went straight to the ground-floor kitchen, padding around the long counter at which in better times the lodge guests relaxed over coffee. Flour and cocoa mix sprinkled the floor. Cupboards exposed, contents spilled out.

In town the brown bears were ornery, too. Kodiakans debated how to minimize the attraction of the municipal dump. A bear just digs *under* a fence, critics said, or the fence just keeps the bears *inside*. What about an electric fence? Skeptics offered eyewitness accounts of clever bears reaching between fence wires to get what they wanted. One man knew of a brown bear that had climbed into an electrified dumpster and was literally *cooking and smoking from the nostrils* but didn't leave.

The townspeople worried that once school started and the kids were out and about, there would be a mauling. After the winter's deep freeze, the spring's cold snap and a salmon return that was as disappointing as the salmonberry crop, the brown bears were hungry and on the prowl. Did the local bear population need thinning? A public meeting was held. A bear guide named Tom Stick proposed a solution: grant more hunting permits to the bear guides.

I had met Tom Stick in December when I helped him to load an outboard motor into a seaplane at Trident Basin, the seaplane base in town. He told me that the Alaska Department of Fish & Game had tried to get him to bring a fall bear hunt to our peninsula to help ease the bear pressure. Nine months a year Stick lived at his hunting lodge in the converted cannery of Port Vita on Raspberry Strait. He was returning now to board it up for the winter. Spectacled, quiet-spoken and underdressed for the cold of December, Stick wasn't anybody's stereotype of a professional bear hunter. He charged ninety-five hundred dollars for a fifteen-day bear hunt and he told me he didn't clear a lot of money at it once he had covered his costs.

Bear hunting is a tightly regulated activity on Kodiak Island. The island's bear population is flourishing, and legal hunting has had a role in the effective management. Frankly the notion of management insults my sense of wilderness, but in the cause of wilderness I have made my peace with management at the expense of wildness. The Kodiak National Wildlife Refuge, nearly two million acres in size, is about as pristine a wilderness as can be had anymore, and bear hunters were among the earliest conservationists to work for protection of the bears in the years leading to the creation of the refuge in 1941. A hunting guide is required for nonresident bear hunters, but even in a guided hunt there is no guarantee of coming away with a brownie, and hunters go home every spring and fall with tags but no bears. Bear hunters are a sporting people with a love of the outdoors, but there is a rowdy sort of bear hunter who weighs on the group's reputation. At the Kodiak Airport I heard a successful bear hunter on the telephone describing his hunt to his girlfriend and serenading her as follows:

"I ain't smoked for three days, honey, and I'm walking kinda high. I'm gonna hide in the house and get my ass fucked up. Yeah, it was a nine-foot-six-inch bear. Way high up the motherfucking mountain. We had our snowshoes out and we slid down and dragged him down on our snowshoes. You'd never believe how steep that was. I had to sleep on the mountain that night, and last night I only slept three hours skinning the hide out. Now don't expect me to go to work right away, honey. I'll see if I can get me a couple of joints first. I guess I wouldn't mind having a cigarette, but if I go back into a smoky room it's gonna be the end of me quitting. Buy me a steak and don't keep me waiting here, huh?"

Kodiak's traditional Alutiit, who hunted the brown bear with bow and arrow or with spear or took them with traps, used the bear for meat, clothing, bedding, tools and decoration, and they considered it disrespectful and inauspicious for a bear hunter to boast about his kill.

By the way, bear guide Tom Stick's hunting camp at Port Vita wasn't immune from brown bear mischief. A bear ripped the door off Stick's new refrigerator just when a party of bear hunters was due. Stick was said to be renovating his lodge kitchen, taking out the cabinets and putting in new vinyl. People gossip about such things in Kodiak. On the radio, at the mail stop, at the boat landing, at the Coast Guard station, or in town at Safeway or King's Diner, people swap bear stories, either their own story or somebody else's, an honest-to-God bear encounter or an unusual sighting—the bear as big as a Winnebago—everybody quick to offer opinions on the best bear defense or the latest bear management plan. A photographer friend of mine, a lover of nature, recently launched a drone into the air to photograph mating brown bears, but the noise of the drone spoiled the romantic atmosphere and the bears uncoupled and fled in opposite directions.

In the brown bears of Kodiak Island, ecotourism and sport hunting and wildlife science have overlapping interests. Each of them contributes to the island's brown bear subculture. Our human fears and vanities, our hypocrisies and generosities are exposed in our dealings with these animals. Everyone here is affected by the brown bears in their legend and in their reality, and life on Kodiak wouldn't be the same without them.

At Cottonwood, our precautions in living with the brown bears have long since become reflexes. We keep a clean cabin, we stay alert, we call aloud in dense vegetation, and we do these things even in quiet years when we rarely see the bears. The brown bears are native to this place, these are their old haunts and trails, and as a rule I defer to them.

The Kodiak brown bear is the shape of the wilderness, a supreme incarnation of nature's power, a vital expression of unseen and omnipresent law. He's a shade of past epochs when fierce and giant creatures roamed the earth, and when I hear the bear or see him, I stop with a slight shudder and look around at my natural home, shaken out of my complacency and returned to my humanity, recognizing myself as a representative man in a wild and glorious country.

fiction

Some Questions Concerning the Discovery of a Dead Donkey

john sperry

WHERE WERE YOU WHEN YOU FOUND THE DONKEY?

Searching for Margo's dog, a gutty dalmador called Twombly—for his spots, like chalk scribbles on furry slate. We had been hiking in the high chaparral several miles from the fire road when the dog bolted. So we whistled and we clicked our tongues, Margo and I, and we called out into the valley floor beneath us into the tops of fir trees and the orthodoxy of distant vineyards. Sixty-million years ago, everything around us, the whole picturesque landscape was nothing but a great warm flux of sea. The dalmador, an avid swimmer, might have appreciated this fact, had he not run off.

At last Twombly returned to us: he was carrying a gift. A tribute rather, since Margo was his master, like the ancient Corsican who traveled to Rome with his beeswax candle. The dog had a bone, cartoonishly large, and our first foolish instinct was to suppose that it was the bone of a dinosaur, some remnant of the fifth extinction, and that we had lucked our way into a treasure horde. After all, hadn't Sotheby's recently sold a nearly complete *Coelophysis* skeleton for $1.5 million? And isn't even a single dinosaur bone worth several thousand dollars?

WHAT DID YOU PLAN TO DO WITH THE MONEY?

Forget the money. I am ashamed to admit that money was my first thought. Had there truly been a dinosaur, we would have magnanimously donated the find to the Petaluma Museum of Natural Science. We coaxed Twombly to the place where he found the bone: instead of a dinosaur, there was the corpse of a hairy quadruped, a beast with a long neck, spindly legs and jackrabbit ears. The corpse was well rotted, though it had no foul odor–or else we did not notice it. We should have known at once that it could have never been a dinosaur, fossils being rare in our part of the continent, because of that great warm flux of prehistoric sea.

"A donkey," Margo said.

Twombly licked tenderly at the donkey's exposed teeth.

A donkey, or rather, the body of a donkey, is such an unlikely object to misplace, to abandon in the high chaparral several miles from the fire road, that the creature must have sensed his doom and wandered out on his own to die in a shade of chamissal.

They are still used by the wineries, sometimes, so he must have climbed up from the valley floor just to die. There is a certain nobility in this ascent, I think, and perhaps this nobility is why a dead donkey presages good luck. When one finds a dead donkey, one must leap over its corpse three times.

Margo explained all of this to me, but the place the donkey had chosen to die—beneath a dense thicket—made it difficult to find a spot from which to execute a leap. Not even the dalmador, a very athletic dog, could have done it. Margo, determined to have the donkey's luck, pulled one of his spindly legs by the hoof out from beneath the thicket. Very little flesh remained, but there was enough for us to properly jump over.

"Hic salta," Margo commanded.

And so we did, three times, while Twombly barked at our antics.

DO YOU KNOW THE DIFFERENCE BETWEEN A DONKEY AND A HORSE?

Only that they're not the same, and that the word "donkey" is a relatively recent coinage, a French epithet for the sophistry of philosophers. During the reign of Louis XIV, the philosophers were always spouting off:

— *Je pense, donc je suis.*
— *Socrate est un homme, donc Socrate est mortel.*
— *Il pleut, donc il pleut.*

Donc, Donc, Donc. Like the braying of a distressed jack.

DO YOU KNOW THE DIFFERENCE BETWEEN A DONKEY AND A MAN?

To be a donkey is to be a beast of burden. It is to give up the free use of one's own musculature in exchange for survival; it is to turn one's body over to be the subject of either perpetual labor or intense violence.

Jean Papire Masson records that Charles IX never met a donkey that he did not kill. In order to show off his physical prowess, each time the king saw a donkey, without fail, he would walk up to it and chop its head off with a single blow from his sword. Why the king did this is left as an exercise for the reader, but he died at the age of twenty-three, a disappointment to his domineering mother.

And then there is the Persian Shah Safi, who once released thirty-two donkeys into a confectionary. The donkeys caused a horrible mess, of course, and then the Shah called for his hunting bow, and he shot some arrows into the donkeys and invited his guests to do the same. Adam Olearius, courtier to the illustrious Duke of Holstein-Gottorp, writes:

—*It was no small amusement to watch the donkeys, riddled with dozens of arrows, gnashing about, covered in jam and powdered sugar, writhing in the strangest manners.*

Later they ate the donkeys, because the Persian Shah Safi considered their flesh a delicacy.

IS THIS VIOLENCE AGAINST DONKEYS UNIQUE?

Hardly. Anecdotes of this sort, if compiled, would fill a large library, or else a small hard drive. Every species of living thing might be represented, save for those strange fishes who haunt the sunless depths of ocean.

If anything, the donkey, because it is a beast of burden, is more than likely to endure the sixth extinction. This is the bargain the beast of burden has obtained: labor in exchange for a chance at survival. Some donkeys reject the terms of this bargain. They throw off their burdens and return to the wild. In Australia, for example, the donkeys of the European colonizers, wishing to find their own high place on which to live and die with nobility, fled their stables and escaped into the floodplains, and there returned to a state of nature. As a result, they are killed by the tens of thousands. They are shot at from helicopters.

If only Charles IX had a helicopter. If only the Persia Shah had a rifle.

But, these are very resourceful donkeys, so what the hunters do is this: they take a young jenny from their farms, and they fit her with a special necklace. It's called a Judas Collar. The jenny is released to wander the desert canyons, to find a herd of wild donkeys. The wild donkeys, thinking that the jenny has, like them, renounced the bargain of the beast of burden, welcome her into their community. They will teach her how to live and die with nobility. It is then that the helicopters appear, having tracked the Judas Collar, and they exterminate the entire herd with their rifles. The jenny is alone allowed to survive, so that she might seek out a new community.

A Judas jenny will not carry on like this forever. After surviving several such extinction events, she comes to associate the society of her kind with the scent of blood and the screams of wounded animals. She is a suspicious of other donkeys, and she is terrified of their companionship. She becomes a loner, and she wanders up into the sandstone peaks to die alone in the quiet scrub, and a new jenny is outfitted with a new collar to take her place.

WHO MOURNS THE FIFTH EXTINCTION?
Nobody.

WHO WILL MOURN THE SIXTH EXTINCTION?
A trick question. Those who survive it will be grateful, those who perish cannot mourn.

AND DID YOUR LUCK CHANGE?
Margo said she was glad to have found the donkey, to have jumped its corpse and taken its luck. Like saluting magpies: a far-off ritual she never thought she'd live to perform. I was inclined to agree with her, but as we walked, I noticed that the dalmador's spots began to shimmer, the boundaries of his spots became less stable, bits of the black wriggling into white. For an instant I thought that I was hallucinating, but kneeling closer, I saw the ticks. They crawled frantically across the dog, dozens of them, each one looking for that perfect site they might call home. Covering his entire body, racing in and out of his ears and along his spine and through his toes, across the gums of his mouth, like a plague of Moses. Ticks are separated into two different families according to how easy they are to squish between one's fingernails, said Margo, but we could not bring ourselves to crush the ticks with our fingernails. Did the ticks flee the donkey's corpse? It could be no coincidence, and yet we struggled to find an explanation. One-hundred and fourteen ticks we found, before we gave up counting.

The Year There Were No Mushrooms

lorraine hanlon comanor

The entire fungus world is wild and unnatural … Sometimes,
when I'm suffocating from an atmosphere of restraint
within myself, I fry them up in butter, with pepper and salt,
and forget where the hurt came from. Instead, I experience
desire creating desire, and then some milder version
of a love that is temporary and guiltless, as if twigs
and bark were giving my life back its own flavor again.

Black Mushrooms
For Seamus Heaney
Henri Cole

How can one ignore a man who keeps you in his heart for fifty years, when he doesn't know where you are or even if you are alive? Initially, I'd dismissed the Facebook friend request, positive it had to be someone else by the same name, until a message arrived referring to specific details of our long-ago time in France. Still, I was unprepared for the call, which I'd almost not answered, being half way out the door with the dog. I can still feel the momentary paralysis when I heard the voice that had always reminded me of Maurice Chevalier's coming over more than nine thousand kilometers of wire, repeating my name, as if he couldn't let go of it. The emotion, which seemed at first too great coming after a hiatus of the better part of a lifetime, left me tongue-tied, wondering if I'd remained a dream to him. Today I can't recall the substance of that first phone conversation, only that it was hard for me to start thinking again in French, the language we'd always used, neither of us proficient in the other's native tongue. Before saying goodbye, he'd pressed to speak again in two days. And after numerous phone calls, I'd agreed to a visit, although still unsure of how we would connect after half a century, what we might have in common.

I'd met Luciano when I was seventeen and he was twenty-four. He was working as a waiter in a hotel in Juan les Pins where I was staying with my mother. She and I were not getting along, I wanting to quit skating and she insisting that I keep on for the Olympics. Ironically, it was she who had pointed him out: "There goes a Greek God," she'd said, unaware that her Greek God was Italian and was tucking little flowers under her daughter's plate when he brought her breakfast croissant. I don't remember how he first approached me, but soon we were sneaking off together to the beach or the nearby woods. He brought a ray of sunshine to my conflicted world and gradually I became dependent on his soft words and warm embrace. After a couple of months, he proposed. At the time, the simultaneous acquisition of a husband and an escape from the ice rink seemed like a good idea. Our ill-conceived plan to run off (I was not yet of age) might have gone forward, had another hotel guest not tipped Mother off to our secret rendezvous. I was immediately on the next flight home to Boston. All communication was forbidden, his letters, I would learn decades later, destroyed before I ever saw them. Was I miserable that fall because I had lost him or because I was back in Boston facing the ice rink? Probably some combination of the two. Convinced I would never see him again and afraid of my parents' threats, I didn't write. We lost contact and after some years both of us married, had families, and later divorced.

At the time of my mother's death, some twelve years ago, I'd found among her papers the tattered corner of one of his envelopes—part of his family name and a street number—and wondered how my life might have evolved had she not interceded. Would a life with such a loving person have made up for the lost education—had we eloped, my parents surely wouldn't have paid for college and medical school—or would I have become frustrated toiling beside him, as he made his way up the restaurant ladder? Never having understood completely what had made him pursue me so ardently, I was surprised now by his describing an afternoon, some years after his divorce, watching television with his daughter. When figure skating had come on and he'd told her that the love of his life had been the American champion, she'd offered to find me.

No longer working in France, he now lived in Ascona, a small town, a stone's throw from his native Italy, on the shores of Lago Maggiore in Ticino, the Swiss canton to the south of Graubünden, where I was training just before I met him. At that time, I'd intended to stay in Switzerland and it was his current hope that I would now return permanently. But much as I loved Switzerland, I was presently rooted in California where my children had been born and raised.

Unwilling therefore to place too much importance on the reunion, I planned to visit friends in Davos before taking the train to Thüsis where he'd offered to pick me up. As I travelled from mountain sleet to valley sunshine, I wondered if meeting was a mistake, whether we'd been better left as a bittersweet memory.

Nevertheless, I stripped my winter jacket down to a V-necked sleeveless top, freshened my lipstick, and tried to look a little less like sixty-seven. As the towns whizzed past, I imagined him in a grey suit at the station, perhaps a bouquet in hand, my heart creeping up in my chest as the train slowed for Thüsis.

There was only one man on the platform. He was not in a grey suit, rather in sweats. Nor was he carrying flowers. And he was smaller than I'd remembered Luciano, but I supposed I had shrunk too. His face was still ruggedly handsome. His once wheat-colored hair, now white, showed no sign of thinning. A smile broke over his face like a wave as he walked towards me and then he hugged me gingerly as if I were some fragile thing. I followed him to his car, wondering if I was really about to drive off with a man I hadn't seen for fifty years. Our conversation was halting. Reluctant to make too many French grammar errors, I focused on the picturesque landscape.

After about an hour, he pulled off the road by a cow pasture. He'd brought a picnic of smoked salmon sandwiches and, as there were no benches, we ate leaning over the fence, taking in the cows—Swiss Browns, as I remember. And then he kissed me gently on the mouth, and my knees wobbled a little, but I stopped short of returning anything passionate. Our sandwiches finished, we climbed back in the car and he started to drive off with the hatchback open. "I'm losing my head over you," he said, getting out to close it. I wasn't yet sure I wanted him to lose his head over me.

Prior to my arrival, he'd cooked for weeks, stocking the freezer, so we would be free to spend afternoons exploring the surrounding alps and valleys rather than hanging out in the kitchen. Each dinner menu offered four or five choices, many of which featured sauces made from mushrooms he'd gathered. One of my favorites was a poplar mushroom sauce for rabbit served over polenta. In Ticino, polenta is cooked in a large copper pot called a paiolo, stirred mechanically for hours, reducing it to a perfect velvet base for a mushroom sauce. September was mushroom season and he, like many Italians, loved to forage.

A mutual love of the outdoors seemed like a promising start, both of us drawn to wild things, but there the commonality ended. A hiking enthusiast, I'd explored the high Sierra trails with my club. The penultimate solo bush-whacker, Luciano detested following the crowd. European mushroom sites are well-guarded secrets, often found above or below the trail on the steepest slopes, some practically vertical. Despite having excellent balance from years of skating, I could imagine a Humpty Dumpty event making my way down these precipices. Neither of us were spring chickens, but as Luciano was seven years older than I, I'd brought only walking shoes, totally inadequate for what he had in mind. Even after taking me out to buy hiking boots, he was quick to announce that certain locations were above my ability. I bit my tongue.

Despite having detested mushrooms as a child—they came in cans with oil and were slimy—I was enthusiastic about mushrooming. I'd gone only once before with the Swiss family I stayed with my year in Graubünden, reluctantly eating that evening's spread, quite surprised to find myself well the next morning. As an anesthesia resident, I'd since witnessed an eastern European family of seven helicoptered into Stanford's ICU, having mistaken Amanita phalloides for a non-poisonous European variety. After a week on life support, they were all dead. I'd developed a healthy respect for fungi.

Still, I was ready to trust Luciano who belonged to a mycology club and had been mushrooming for years, never hesitant to leave behind a specimen about which he had even the slightest doubt. Fortunately, the mushrooms we were after had distinctive features: the brilliant gold of chanterelles, the decorated caps of Massa di Tamburo, the hoof-like clumps of pieds de mou-tons, the dome-shaped cap and underside sponge-like pores of boletus, the thick tubular stipe of their king, known here as porcini. Different varieties, I learned, gravitated to different trees: oak, ash, chestnut, alder, beech, pine, and fir.

My initial mycology lesson took place near his home in a section of wood along the River Maggia he called the enchanted forest, not just because of the moss-covered stone walls that wove through its trees, but also because it was home to a wide range of mushrooms. Luciano was intrigued by all varieties, even non-edible ones.

He foraged with a hiking stick, a cloth bag in his rucksack, a basket in the car trunk, and an open Swiss Army knife ready to clean a specimen on site. In a minefield of tree roots, I was reluctant to walk with an open knife. Cleaning could wait until we got home, but he would frown when I emptied a sack of dirty mushrooms on the kitchen table.

At first, he would stop me when we were hunting, telling me to slow down and look around so that I might find what he'd already spotted, praising highly my initial successes. But he seemed most pleased when I noticed a specimen that had escaped him. While he criticized my lack of skill with the knife, he was quick to compliment my keen eye. But while he maintained we should search in different locations, he got quite cross if I wandered too far afield. He was, after all, responsible for me.

Still, we worked well in this teacher-student relationship. He was sensitive about my superior education and here was an area where he was the expert and I was the novice. He would point out the defining features of each mushroom, explaining whether it was a look-a-like, but not the real thing, whether it was too damp or old for harvesting, its leg most likely filled with worms.

I was an apt pupil, gradually acquiring a French mycology vocabulary and anticipating an afternoon of foraging as I might an Easter egg hunt. There was an endorphin high associated with each edible find, be it the brown cap of a boletus or the gold appendage of a chanterelle. In addition to having a sharp eye from hunting lizards as a child, spotting mushrooms utilized other skill sets of mine, ones that might be described as a knack for "Where's Waldo?" or what my pathologist colleagues referred to as "match the wallpaper."

Mushrooming became our prime activity. When we came home from a good haul, we'd take some photos, open a bottle of Proseco, and get right to work cleaning. If the majority were past their prime, Luciano would set me to slicing them thin, laying them out on trays to dry on the balcony. If they were fresh, he would send me to the garden for parsley, while he put on what I considered kitschy Sicilian love songs. Then he'd sauté them up with garlic and just a touch of oil, as he liked them crispy, and the kitchen would take on a woody aroma. If we'd been lucky enough to find a porcini, he'd make a Carpaccio, arranging the slices in a pinwheel—"You eat first with your eye," he told me—before spritzing them with a fine olive oil and a crack of pepper. The salad had a nutty flavor. It was like eating the forest, he said.

Many times at dinner, he would praise his own sauce and I would agree politely, knowing more of a response was expected, yet unable to come up with something substantive about its rich texture or subtle flavors. Just how many times was I expected to say how good it was? It was the same thing with his art. His first painting, a basket of porcini, hung next to the dining room table. "Not many people could have done such a good job with those mushrooms," he said. "Look at the way the light hits the caps." Again, I agreed politely, still not coming up with a credible-sounding compliment. What was remarkable to me was not the painting per se, but that he had taught himself by studying the masters in Europe's museums. "You're a miser with compliments," he said, just as he'd previously complained I avoided terms of endearment. But when we had a good haul of mushrooms, these issues rarely came up. We were simply too occupied with the harvest.

During my first visits, mushrooms seemed to follow us wherever we travelled from his neighboring Valle Maggia south to the isle of Elba where we found hundreds of what the locals call pinaioli, a type of boletus that grows under the island's pines. We collected so many that we had to scavenge discarded boxes from markets, setting up drying racks on the balcony of our hotel room, over the bidet in the bathroom, the hair dryer running day and night. Our conversations revolved around where we might search next, how to create more drying room, the different dishes we would make. The only possible hiccup was when he would send me into town to beg for another box in my faltering Italian.

While I was happy in the role of student, and he seemed content to teach, occasionally I would worry about how I was contributing aside from paying for some groceries and cleaning up the Ascona kitchen. But the concern usually passed at the conclusion of another successful hunt. Mushrooming became a highlight of my year, so much so that after a couple of visits I left a pair of hiking boots in his closet.

Then one year there were no mushrooms and things went south. While California had been subject to an El Niño winter, Europe had experienced a drought. Where the previous year there were more mushrooms than we could handle, now there were none to be found.

Mushrooms had a mind of their own, Luciano explained. Even in their season, it was impossible to predict where or when they might appear. Some insisted the new moon brought them out. Often they cropped up in the same place several years in a row, only to disappear the following year. Mushrooming required patience. Sometimes you were lucky, sometimes not, but you always had to have an eye out and to be prepared.

As we searched stands of pines and chestnuts to no avail, I began to think about relationships in mycological terms. Good ones, I believed, were like the mychorrizal symbiosis between the mushroom and its chosen tree where the mushroom surrounds the tree's root tips with mycelia, not only protecting the tree from disease, but also providing it with carbohydrates in exchange for the tree's nutrients. To date, our relationship seemed closer to commensalism than mutualism, my being the recipient of his knowledge and hospitality. Without my verbalizing it, my concern had not escaped Luciano. "And what are you contributing?" he'd asked, when annoyed with something I'd done. If I were the tree, I wasn't giving back much by the way of nutrients. Not that I hadn't tried to reciprocate when he'd visited me in California, but he hadn't enjoyed my group hikes and barbeques, and so I'd decided that if our relationship were to continue, it best stay in Europe. But regardless of its location, I needed to tip the contribution scale.

A possible opportunity arose during that year's trip to Elba. To add to the disappointment of no mushrooms, Luciano had come down with a miserable cold.

"Un coup de froid from the air conditioning," he complained, taking to bed the first day back on the island, as I kept a respectful distance. "You're behaving like I had the plague."

"No reason for both of us to be sick," I'd countered. The doctor me could look after him, while setting him straight about colds. As he claimed to be open to new ideas, I added, "Your sore throat and congestion are not from the air conditioner. You have a virus and it's contagious."

This information went against Italian folklore. It was almost worse than my suggesting that his diagnosis of diabetes of shock, that followed his learning of his wife's affair, was probably twenty years in the making, insulin resistance often taking that long to develop. "I like my doctor's explanation better. Swiss doctors are just as good as American doctors, maybe even superior," he'd retorted. "My ex gave me this disease."

I promptly took off my doctor hat, deciding to limit my physician role to pharmacy runs for the Italian remedies he requested.

As Luciano felt better, we walked sections of the island. He tried to teach me jokes, but, as someone who believed humor could not be memorized, I was a poor student. After a while, he gave up and concentrated on taking pictures, which he reviewed immediately on arriving back at the hotel, purportedly asking for my opinion on the captured details or the intensity of the colors, before posting them on Facebook. Later, I would watch him tally the "I like its," feeling guilty about my inability to offer sufficient praise and simultaneously annoyed by his reliance on Facebook kudos. What kept me from giving the positive reinforcement he so desperately needed? The amount he required or my reluctance to reward what I considered narcissistic behavior?

I was actually relieved when he switched subjects from jokes and photos to family tensions so, instead of feeling pressed for a compliment, I could encourage him to pick up the phone, not to lose contact with a child keeping their distance. But while I was giving lip service to closer relationships, he claimed my arms-length demeanor was ruining his vacation. Dinners, where we'd normally discuss the menu, did not fare better than the walks. The hotel dining room was crowded and noisy, rowdy Italian conversations on one side of us, guttural German ones on the other. I missed some of his comments. "You're deaf," he concluded. "You need your ears washed out."

What I needed was a good rainstorm to bring out the mushrooms, or so I thought. But when it arrived, it produced no results. There were simply no mushrooms that fall.

The spring brought no morels either and when I returned, his family experienced a series of crises: his ex-brother-in-law committed suicide, his son-in-law fell into another bout of depression, his son's significant other had a cardiac arrest. In response to the question of why the heart of a forty-year-old would suddenly stop, I offered possible explanations of myocardial infarct, cardiomyopathy, cerebral vascular accident, possibilities he deemed unnecessarily grim and which prompted a laundry list of my faults: negativity being foremost (I even reported the weather in terms of percent chance of rain), stinginess with compliments and terms of endearment, a close second, (traits that went along with the chilly Anglo temperament, which also gravitated to Baroque music over Italian opera), memory lapses, clumsiness with locks, unwillingness to assume responsibility beyond sous-chef in his kitchen (he'd decided Americans relied on fast food), refusal to speak Italian (if he could speak five languages, surely I could manage a fourth). Miffed, I focused on his irritating traits: tendency to criticism, a Pollyanna approach to life, constant need of applause, lack of interest in books, films, or politics, TV viewing limited to snooker and NCIS, frequent imitations of native English speakers having a go at his language—a practice that had kept me from uttering a word of his melodic Italian in his presence.

I began to look forward to his siesta, when I had a half an hour to myself to read or write, but even these stolen minutes caused issues, because when he awoke, I would often be mid-sentence and slow to respond to a request to review that morning's photos. Instead of concentrating on them, I would be thinking of our afternoon walk, hoping we might find even one mushroom. I'd become used to taking home Ziplocs filled with dried specimens, which I would use in various recipes over the winter. But hope as I might, we didn't find even one that season, and on returning to his kitchen, we skipped the Proseco.

The more he maintained that one didn't need mushrooms for a nice walk, the more I became convinced our relationship depended on their presence (doomed if that were the case) and the more I focused on our incompatibilities. As if he could read my mind, he told me there was no such thing as the perfect man. I started counting the days until my scheduled flight back to the States at which time I would ask for space.

Perhaps not surprisingly, my carefully worded letter, sent several weeks later, missed its mark. How could I feel ill at ease after all he'd done for me? He expressed his love but would not beg me to return. I let things sit, avoiding phone calls, minimizing emails.

At Christmas, I was surprised by a box of dried porcini he'd purchased in Italy. Despite the drought, a limited area in northern Tuscany had received enough rain to produce a few of the prized species. As he said, mushrooms had a mind of their own. Sometimes you were lucky, sometimes not.

Opening the package, I caught a whiff of the enchanted forest and found myself back in his kitchen, cleaning that morning's harvest, anticipating that evening's delicious dish. Having exhausted my supply of dried mushrooms a few months before, I hadn't made any of his recipes recently, but now I was eager to use his gift. When my kids arrived for the holiday, I made a mushroom risotto. I added the dried porcini to a turkey and barley soup. Then I pulverized twenty grams to enhance a tomato sauce, although unsure of how to duplicate the one he often served with rabbit. On a roll, I expanded my efforts to his other plates that didn't feature mushrooms. I treated the family to his brasato with polenta, marinating the beef two days in a cabernet, only I didn't have a paiolo and I only stirred the polenta for half an hour. It was not as creamy as his. I tried to emulate his minestrone, but even pancetta was no substitute for his smoked beef base. I followed his lasagna recipe to a tee, but my crust was not quite as crispy as his. Still, every dish I made the children devoured. But once they went back to their own lives, the few remaining leftovers didn't taste the same eating them alone.

As the months passed, I began to wonder if, like mushrooms, some relationships could be seasonal. Differences that might make a full-time commitment challenging might be overcome for shorter periods of time. Rather than continuing to search for better ways to contribute, I revisited his list of complaints, believing change would have to start with me. After all, he'd had seven more years to become set in his ways.

While change in what had now become my eighth decade was a tall order, I planned to start with the easy fixes, as had been my habit addressing editorial comments on medical manuscripts. On first review of his complaint list, there didn't appear to be any. It was unlikely I would change the way I answered medical questions. I would probably never be a great compliment-giver or a genius with locks. Short-term memory might be improved with mnemonics, writing more things down, but was not guaranteed. That left Italian. Although I couldn't imagine us abandoning our comfortable French, maybe he would appreciate even a small effort. My son was in a language school in Turino. I could join him for a couple of weeks.

But even as I memorized verb conjugations, I still worried that the relationship was mushroom-dependent. I found myself hoping that, given the year's normal precipitation to date, the autumn might bring a fine crop. Before boarding the train to Ticino, I began checking the long-term weather outlook for the region. Where last fall I'd reported the forecast as percent chance of rain, I now began to think of it in terms of percent chance of sunshine, as mushrooms also require the heat of the sun to bring them out.

Several days after my arrival back in Ascona, we returned to the enchanted forest. The air smelled of mulch, the ground spongy beneath my feet due to recent rain. However, the last few days had brought intermittent rays of afternoon sun to the forest floor. Barely five minutes into our walk, alongside a tree stump, I spotted the familiar cap of a boletus. And then another buried in the moss. Around the corner was a whole family of yellow jacks. I opened the Swiss army knife Luciano had given me and cut away the dirt from a stem. He nodded his approval, while pointing out a black trumpet, a variety I hadn't seen before. We filled two bags with boletus and Massa di Tamburo for the upcoming family get-together. His son-in-law was doing better. His son's significant other had made a miraculous recovery.

During his afternoon siesta, I spread out our haul and started slicing caps and legs, laying them out on a paper towel to dry, as I'd been taught, saving the freshest to cook immediately. When he woke, I asked, "Mi insegnerai a fare una buona salsa?" "Certo," he said, surveying the ingredients I'd assembled: stock, tomato concentrate, garlic, and white wine. "A good start, but you forgot the rosemary," he said, taking a chilled bottle of Proseco out of the fridge, as I reached for a sauté pan. I nodded, smiling, as I spritzed the surface with olive oil and turned up the heat.

[sweet/alyssum]

(for Derick W. Burleson)

michele n. harmeling

[sweet alyssum and borage in azure bloom in the salad the farm feeds the
people who live here and twenty-nine other families]
–Derick W. Burleson, July 2008

If I owned twenty-nine acres of land what could
 be done with all that bloom under azure sky?
Sweet cut-grass chaff rising

after mower's rotating blades.
Simple cuts-chlorophyll

and drying hay and musk of a few horses.

The farm would feed my people: whomever
gathers to live on purple potato,

on bitter baby greens, white alyssum.
On each other, dropping silver hairs into the carved

wood salad bowl. Sharing water dipper, sharing beds.

 If I gather spring borage, who would eat it?
Who eats the mushrooms I bring now,

pock-capped, spongy undersides, creamy icicles
grown from rotting but still-standing birch? Silage

of Sitka valerian, fern fiddleheads, and dark

brown chaga conks, wrested from trunk and boiled down.
White alyssum on the windowsill, silver

mushroom knife in hand. Yes, whomever gathered to live
on this farm would eat well. Horses whickering for garden

carrots as sky darkens to azure. What Magic is it

to feed other people, to use one's hands as tillers,
to turn up from glacial loam an elixir on which to live?

fiction

Fishing
joanneh nagler

At four a.m. I rise and put the coffee on. I don't drink coffee, but it doesn't matter. The electrical currents in my brain that cause me to move habitually, mesmerizing me with automatic movement, are embedded so strongly in place that the pot is two-thirds full before I remember: the coffee drinker is gone.

I pad through the house and let the stuff cook until it burns, letting the kitchen and living room fill with the rubbery, metallic odor of it—some sort of justice in the vengeance of it. Then I remember my mother's commentary on being left: "Jillian, resentment is a poison you swallow hoping the other person will die."

I turn back towards the kitchen, unplug the pot, and carry it, barefooted, across the gravel driveway to the trashcan. The icy, late-autumn Minnesota morning pierces me, my feet sharply needled by tiny, chewed-up rocks. The sky is blacker than I remember it being at this hour, my small lake town covered by a pall of darkness.

I nurse a secret truth as I walk—a dreadful and appalling one, and not just in this moment, either, but each night as I lie in bed: *I hope it's me who dies.* Not to spite him, not even to hurt him or make him pay, but just because I've had *enough.* I'm worn thin, wrung out by months and months of yearning for things to somehow right themselves, pretending that they will. I'm limp and exhausted and feel no shame in admitting that I don't care anymore.

I have refused to cry—a rebellion that is not helping me—the weight of holding in my grief like walking with huge stones strapped to my body.

I catch my reflection in the uneven glass of the tool shed's battered, wood-framed window as I pass, coffee maker in hand. My hair is matted and thrown to one side; my face looks drawn and pulled downward as if gravity had grown weightier overnight. My clothes hang limply from my limbs, having not been changed in days.

I approach our giant, empty black trash bin—which I grudgingly admit I have never been able to move to the curb without his help—open it and let it fall: pot, hot coffee, electrical wiring and apparatus. It's self-pity at its finest.

I stand and stare at the morass of mess in the can, the broken glass shattered over cord, plastic, and burnt coffee, now below my reach, and consider the lazy-Susan-sampler-plate of what I could use today to absent my head from my own unraveling self. I ponder the options: alcohol—I can't keep it down; food—I'm already nauseous; drugs—I don't have any; shopping—I hate it; or sex—*hardly.*

I sniff the icy air meanly—I have no choice but to feel every ounce of my own sinewy pain today.

My bare toes are frozen to the gravel, and as I begin to move, little pieces of rock prick at my skin and lacerate the bottom of my feet in a staccato, pin-sharp needling. A glint of bare street light streaks into the shed as I pass, the door ajar where I left it five days ago when he emptied out the last of his tools and junk. All at once I want to throw up, and I steady myself on the door jamb.

The wave of nausea passes, and as I turn to go my eyes settle upon my father's thirty-year-old fishing gear stashed in a dusty corner of the shed. I stare momentarily.

"I will go fishing then," I say out loud to no one.

In the freezing cold pre-dawn, it feels like a century since I fished—I remember it's literally been a quarter-century—and I find I do not remember how to begin.

I move towards my father's gear, and like spying a pinhole of light in a pitch-black room, the fog that has been clogging my brain is pinpricked a bit—a tiny pressure release in the balloon of my loss—and as I reach for his ancient, closeted rods, I see a broad, handsome man with a shock of black-and-grey streaked hair standing over my ten-year-old self, teaching me how to push a nightcrawler through a fishhook.

"It wasn't called a *fishhook*," I say out loud as I finger the rod. I feel a sharp stab at my left temple, realizing I have forgotten the language of this. I know worms and hooks and fishing line, but I have lost the delicate finesse of the detailed vocabulary that my father taught me. The words fall flat as I say them—"rod," "line," "hook"—my generic knowledge leaving me bereft, as if in my adult life I should have loved what he loved and learned what he knew.

I want to be near him now, the father who truly loved me and would not have sought his own escape from me under any earthly circumstance, yet died and left me anyway. I pick up a flashlight from the floor, balancing it and shining it upwards, and begin gathering all that I can of his fishing gear.

There are three poles—a shiny black one which appears grey at first, covered with dust and cobwebs; a severely cracked blond wooden relic; and a polished burnt orange one which was once the exact metallic hue of my first Stingray bicycle.

My father bought the pole the same day he bought my bike, coordinating the colors so that they would match.

"Jillie! Jillie! Close your eyes!" he said to me. "Come on now. Close 'em! Okay, okay. Now *look!*" He pulled the orange Stingray from around our Ford Station wagon and lifted it upright with his left hand, holding the fishing rod up in his right like the torch on the Statue of Liberty.

"Look what I found! A matching pole and bicycle! Our favorite things, Jillie—yours and mine!"

Tears sting my eyes as I stand in the shed, remembering him, and I pull the orange rod to my chest—a sharp and withered replacement for the father who would have held me on this day, who would have let me bury my grief against his thickening belly and shoulders.

I force myself to move and reach—to try at least—and I beat back spider webs and falling pieces of cracked ceiling tile to free the rest of the gear. There are the other two rods, a tackle box, some buckets, a couple of nets, some waders, and a knife for filleting. I am amazed to find that much of the stuff still looks functional.

I have no recollection of lines or how they work or what one must do to prepare them. I figure I'll just take all the rods as they are and hope against reason that one of them will still work, reeling itself out into the stream as if it knows what it's doing.

I stare at the gear, and suddenly I have no faith whatsoever that I can do this. I feel *called*—that's all: as if some invisible force could lift me from the desperation of my self-neglect with a thin thread of hope held together with fishing line.

I make myself a breakfast of whole-wheat rolls and good cheese, apples and tea, and wrap it all into a basket. I know it is wishful thinking to assume that I will eat, but I take it anyway. I pack the gear and the food in the car, start the engine and steer towards the highway.

My father would have stopped, on the mornings we fished, for doughnuts and coffee on the way out of town at a little café called Gert's, which opened at five a.m. and served only homemade pastries.

"Wanna little something?" Gert would say to me with a warm, yellow-toothed smile. She wore a fishnet atop wound-up grey hair that pulled into a peak over her forehead, and a white apron stained with frosting.

I would point to a giant tray of huge, glaze-covered cinnamon rolls, warm from the oven and dripping with sugary frosting, and she'd pop one onto a paper plate and wrap it in tin foil. The cinnamon roll was as big as the plate and three inches high, and it would take me all morning on the riverbed to eat it, my father smiling at me each time I took a bite, as if his little treat to me was all I would ever need to find happiness.

Gert's—now a second-hand store with a crumbling exterior—flies by on the left side of my driving sightline, and the ratty Goodwill fare in the window snaps my heart into broken, dry reeds.

A little farther on, I turn past the main lake that situates our town, and then take a sharp, curved left onto a one-lane county road. I take the banked turn quickly the way my father used to—a crack-the-whip-in-the-car effect that used to always make me laugh out loud.

I swerve a little, and then check my face in the rear-view mirror. No laughing today.

I travel the next seventeen miles to the river in near-darkness, my headlights not nearly enough to lift the weighing blackness of the sky. At the junction of a sandy, dirt road I pull over to a little battered shack on the downside of a rural intersection. No one is around, but as I open the door, I see a white plastic pail with a tight, sealed cover, and inside it, several Styrofoam containers of night crawlers. I open one of the Styrofoam cups just to check—wet dirt and crawling things—and I notice that I'm surprised to find them alive. I leave five dollars in an empty pail and take my cargo back to the car.

Twenty years ago, old Alfred Nebus would have been here at this hour, shaking my father's hand and talking over the floating abilities of various kinds of bait.

"Alfred! What's the good word?" my father would say to him. Alfred was over eighty, a retired farmer, and had spent a lifetime fishing the streams and lakes in our county.

"White bass are runnin', Bill. That's the good word!" He'd bend down creakily towards me and say something sweet like, "You're gonna be a *fisher-woman* when you grow up, and a damned *good* one, now aintcha?"

I'd nod and he'd pull a handful of lollypops out of his pants pockets for me and let me chose my color. I chose green every time—my father's favorite. He and Alfred would laugh, and Alfred would say, "She loves you somethin' terrible, Bill. You know that, don'tcha?"

"Sure do, Alfred. Love her more, though."

Today, it's a miracle to me that the little shack still stands, and I bless the son or niece or grandchild of Alfred's who leaves me these night crawlers, these gifts.

The darkness has finally broken into a pink and windy dawn, and I breathe a little lighter now. I hate the dark. As a child I had terrible nightmares for a time which resurfaced so vehemently in the three months prior to my husband's leaving that I awoke screaming several nights a week. Yet my eyes would blink awake in the morning, wide open and full of the denial of another nebulous day.

"He's told you he's in love with someone else, so you know what's coming, don't you?" my therapist had said to me.

"So what?" I had retorted, rebelliously pushing back. "Knowing doesn't help a damn thing. It just makes the inevitable leaving more drawn out." I had been right.

Three minutes later I am at the stream, shaking out my father's waders, fearing tarantulas and black widows—though I know this is not their latitude—or June bugs and beetles—though it's late fall, almost winter. Nothing seems logical to me anymore. Nothing adds up. I fear things that don't exist. I pretend that what's happening isn't. I refuse to see what's right in front of me.

I stare at the water, momentarily frozen. "Huh," I say to no one, "I have no idea what I'm fishing for."

I set up the orange pole first, hook a nightcrawler, reel out the line. It creaks, but miraculously it works. The wooden pole sticks and jams, nothing doing. But the shiny black pole lets out its line effortlessly, as if it had been waiting for my unsteady hands to give it another chance to reach into the purplish-green, rushing water. I stick the butts of both poles into the edge of the soft streambed and reach for my thermos.

November, I think to myself. *What runs in winter?* This place was my father's favorite when the white bass were running. *Was that spring or autumn?* I am struck by how grief has obliterated my memory. My reference points have faded and jumbled, and I feel awash with no firm ground to stand upon. *Was it Spring?*

"It's the best time ever, Jillie—you put your line in, and you pull out a fish! It'll give you *fishing fever.*" My father had flashed me his favorite grin, the one he knew lit up the room and weakened me to do whatever he wanted me to do. It was our secret joy: me holding out on some pleasure of his, and him slowly convincing me, his exuberance in swaying me over drawing him out in loud, boisterous assertions of "fevers" and "the greatests" and "best evers."

Suddenly I am stricken, bent over with the sharp pointedness of agony stuck in my chest—the places my father touched in me, all at once ravaged and on fire with my need for him. That someone should *care* that I have the "best time ever" knocks me to my knees and I am weeping on the cold earth.

"Come *back!*" I yell out loud, pounding the ground with my fists, face-down in the weeds and mud. "God*damn* it, come back!!"

I cry in heavy sobs, my shoulders collapsed around my heart like a fallen deer with an arrow in its flank. My muscles give way to the frozen ground, and my hands reach for the dirt. I cannot hold myself up any longer. Rivulets pour from my face and wet the soil, snot and gasps caught in the icy grass. I rise momentarily to vomit in the weeds, and then fall again, giving up.

I find it shocking that the break in the dam of my grief should be borne alone, that the pouring out of its depths are plummeted by this wholly solitary moment, and while I know no one will be coming from out of the underbrush to hold me or save me, the child in me still wants it. *Please! Where is my father when I need him?* I cry. *I want him to come back!*

After a long time I rise, not knowing what force will make me stand again, and wipe my face.

I stare out over the water. Something is different. The light has changed, the stream has colored into a bright blue-green in the early morning sun, and my lines—both of them—have bites. My heart beats quickly; I am not sure which line to reel in first. I reach for the orange one, and in two seconds I am fighting with the line—more from the wake of the stream's current than the weight of the fish—and as I draw it out of the water I see what it is: a white bass.

I see a large school of them below my feet, and for a moment my breath goes out of me. I reel in the second line, re-bait, cast, pull in another. I spend all morning baiting and catching, a rhythm of completeness that overtakes my grief and blots out my numbness. I fill my buckets, my plastic bags, my breakfast basket. There are more bass than I can count.

"I'm sure there's a limit on the lot of you," I say to a particular fish, "but I don't care."

It must have been spring when we fished, my father and I. It seems like that should have been when it was, when fish would school towards the surface, mate, and begin again.

I feel a thin thread of certainty returning to my limbs as I pack the car with my loot: these fish, all of these white bass that should not be running in November. My face in the car window looks different—piqued with what? *Interest.* My face looks *interested.*

The engine hesitates, sputters, then starts, and I sense a movement in my heart, a mysterious beating. My father is near. In the car, the smell of fish is suddenly everywhere.

As I drive my face creases into the first small smile I have smiled in months. I will eat the fish all winter and spring will come.

poem

Bell Lap Anaerobic
heikki huotari

Some of you with birthdays are not young
and if I knew that you were coming in your white
coats for me I would not have baked that cake. Your
tongue will taste the air in vain, there'll be no
melting snowflake and no sibling to outrage, so
while the organist is playing, Joyful Joyful, in
staccato, bring your atavisms to the altar so they
may be saved. The souls of crows are taking steps,
bad-acting, each in some way pantomiming, *I don't
care what I bend mentally as long as it's a spoon.*

Estate Sale

derek updegraff

Driving, Andrea makes out an Estate Sale sign at her neighborhood's entrance. She doesn't think much of it. Her mind drifts while the car heads home. Did she pack the kids' snacks in their front pouches? Yeah, she did. Would she want sex tonight? Maybe. She's ovulating and nostalgic. Just yesterday she had to go through Sandy's drawers again and box up more toddler clothes he's growing out of.

She passes more Estate Sale signs. She turns her turn. Another sign pops up, its arrow directing her to where she was already going. She veers onto Laredo, and there's the last sign, hammered into the lawn of her across-the-street neighbor.

She figures Mrs. Harrington must be dead. How did she not know this? How many days ago—weeks ago—did that happen? Her walkway roses have been looking a little dry recently. She kills the ignition, steps down from her mid-size, drifts across the street. She's drawn into her dead neighbor's house. Some woman says, "Welcome. Just opening up." Some man says, "Take a look around."

Andrea looks around. She cradles things in her palms: porcelain cups, figurines, antique school bells. She flips through records, fingers books. She studies church directories, watching the Harringtons age together each year until Mrs. Harrington's alone in the last few.

She sits in chairs, brushes fingers over a sewing machine. No room's off limits. She approaches the master bed. It's only a double. They would have had to touch a lot while sleeping. The closet is open. The clothes are tagged too. His clothes are gone, sold off or donated some years back. She pulls a dress off the hanger, sniffs musk, puts it back beside the peach jumpsuit Mrs. Harrington would wear when watering her roses. She moves to the dresser, opens one drawer, then another. The bottom drawer is full of lace. Doilies, she thinks. But she pulls out the fabric, and a camisole unfolds. A real sexy number. And so intricate. Floral stitching. Leaf-size holes to reveal slices of skin while the full sheen sections corralled breasts and buttocks. Each item seems to have been sewn by Mrs. Harrington, a collection of lingerie forged from tablecloths and doilies. Andrea clears out the drawer, gathering the softness in her arms.

In the living room the woman is greeting new passersby. The man is sitting at a card table with a little register. Andrea wonders if this man and woman are the Harringtons' children, here now to sell their parents' furniture, their mother's knickknacks.

Andrea lays down the bundle of homemade lingerie on the table. She asks, "How much?"

The man says, "Oh my, is that… I don't think we marked that."

"How's twenty?" she asks. "Forty?" She coaxes two bills from her front pocket and floats them to his table. "They're good quality," she says, holding up a pair of panties stitched from doilies.

He's dazed, probably thinking of Mrs. Harrington in new light, perhaps gaining some insight into his recently passed mother.

Andrea corrals the mass of lingerie in her arms again. She gestures toward the bills on the table. She asks, "Good? Are we good?"

The man says, "Okay."

She's through the door and across the street. She's laying the items on her bed. She undresses and inches into the cream one with magnolias, careful not to tear any of the fine stitching. She fills it. It holds her well in the places it holds. She walks around her bedroom in Mrs. Harrington's homemade lingerie, now hers. She's not encumbered. She moves like running water. She's thinking about her own mother, remarried, probably many years away from being alone. She's thinking about her children, what they'll make of her when they're clearing out her drawers one day, rummaging through her things with tags in hand. And she's thinking about her husband, what he'll think of the carefully stitched magnolias when she undresses tonight and pulls him to her.

She slides her clothes back on over Mrs. Harrington's lingerie. Then she puts the remaining items in her drawers, integrating them in with her own clothes, happy to have found such lovely things as these.

In the end,

devon balwit

I shoveled you to the curb, dustpan jumbling
your meticulous hoarding of decades. What could
be sold was spared, but the rest, the memorabilia,
was spilled from drawers, yanked from shelves.
I had jackboots on. I silenced.

Day after day, I dismembered you and bagged
the pieces. The cat would not come out
from under the bed until we took the bed,
and then we bagged the cat, and the stray pill
that rolled out beside.

The empty house settled about its fracture,
the cracks in the wall stretching from molding
to floor. The unmown grass crowded the fence
like the stunned of Andersonville. No longer
son or husband, never a father, you became nothing.

Not wholly true. Like one who grabs a handful
of earth on pilgrimage, I pocketed a journal
from your teens, some photographs, investing them
with mana: the Midwest that shaped you,
the Swiss slopes that cradled your forebears.

Mirage

gabriela denise frank

our family and friends
lost blackbirds   squawking unintelligibly

My body   shrouded   a forgotten wad
no   time

remaining

for another sweaty embrace.

I curse the fucking sun

the yawning   day

I'm tempted to shrug

my bad manners   she is still
there, though she isn't

everything is wrong today
the   earth   swallowed by my mother

into the stout green grass

two months ago   Mom was still alive

I squint   kicking   scuffing

running

in a cemetery filled with dead strangers

burnt yellow at the edges

stab a trail of divots into   Dad leaning against Mom

in a black pearly-button shirt

I sneer
such a strong girl

I haven't
cried
so strong   I want to scream

I am a coward   Would Mom be proud of that?

I don't care   burn
away my skin and bones   I   want to die

we

abandon   my mother's body

A lovely woman.
A shame.
thinnest   praise
my mother's good china   never used

tiny cups
and
black
needles poking   through the snow

my strange fantasy

my mother's funeral
all in my head
the dream
A   parallel course

how young
she was   the weight of   living
turns out   I *don't* want to disappear

silently   swiftly   that inevitable
conclusion   foolish wishes of   grief

come true

I sway back and forth on the freshly mown turf grass with what is left of our family and friends. We flock like lost blackbirds, milling on the too-perfect lawn, squawking unintelligibly. Our dark clothes are too hot even though it is December, even though a freak snowstorm blanketed the desert overnight.

It is nearly noon, and the temperature in Sun City, Arizona, creeps upwards toward the piercing blue sky.

It is 1990. I am sixteen.

My body is shrouded in a wrinkled A-line dress—a forgotten wad at the back of my closet that no one had time to iron for me. The black cotton radiates an overwhelming heat that I cannot escape by breathing or by fanning myself with the xeroxed missalette. Mom's best friend, Louise, is wearing a smear of chalky watermelon-pink lipstick, a colorful shout in contrast with her ebony sack dress, which is nearly as wrinkly as mine. The waxy pink makeup melts into the cracks of her lips like the scant clumps of remaining snow leak into the scrubby bases of the live oaks that twist upward from the cemetery grounds. I turn away as Louise draws me into her freckled bosom for another sweaty embrace.

My asthmatic lungs pant at the humidity. I curse the fucking sun, thrilling myself by thinking the F-word. After ten years in Arizona—we moved from Detroit to Phoenix when I was six—I should be accustomed to the yawning mercury shifts between day and night, but I never could acclimate to the delta between bone-dry chill and sweltering heat, from tar-black night to blinding day.

"Ready to go?" Louise asks, squeezing my shoulders. A halo of sweat glistens at the hairline of her carrot-red perm. I'm tempted to shrug off her moist, plump arm. It's too warm for her body to press against mine. I imagine Mom scolding my bad manners. Somehow, she is still there, even though she isn't. I feel guilty for my silent intolerance of kind, sweet Louise.

"I think she's ready to go," Louise whispers loudly to my grandmother.

Lost in thought, or prayer, Nanny ignores Louise, a snub unbefitting her classic steel-wool stoicism. But everything is wrong today. Nanny stares down at Pop's gray granite headstone, situated a few feet from the open mouth of earth that has swallowed my mother's body. All the grave markers in Sunland Memorial Park are the same: polished low-profile rectangles sunk evenly into the stout green grass. Nothing regal, like the old churchyards back east. The date on the left of Pop's headstone reads July 1910; the date on the right reads October 1990. When we stood here two months ago to bury my grandfather, Mom was still alive.

I don't have the energy to look at Louise's freckled face, or return her sympathetic gaze, which I feel trained on mine. Instead, I squint down, kicking a bare patch of lawn, scuffing the toe of my patent leather dress-up shoe because there's no one around to tell me not to. I block out every sound except the electric whirr of golf carts whizzing by, and the faraway buzz of lawnmowers trimming the green. Sunland Memorial is located in the heart of a 55-and-over master-planned golf course community where golf carts are street-legal and the speed limit is 35. I used to love running errands with Pop in his golf cart when I stayed overnight with him and Nanny. That morning, we buried Mom next to Pop in the veterans' section because burying her elsewhere, in a cemetery filled with dead strangers, sounded lonelier than any of us could bear.

The humid aroma of cut grass hangs in the air. It makes me sneeze in violent bursts. The too-bright sun glares. The incessant cooing of mourning doves—too-whit? too-whoo!—gives me a pounding headache. Hot staccato gusts blow the high palm fronds sideways, like American flags, burnt yellow at the edges. I fall into the wind to see if it will catch me. It doesn't.

Louise clears her throat. She says to my grandmother, more forcefully this time, "I think she's ready to go home."

I walk over and sling my arm through Nanny's. We ignore Louise, who puts her hand on my sweaty back as we walk away. The kitten heels of my shoes, the ones Mom bought me for prom that spring, stab a trail of divots into the turf. We find Dad leaning against Mom's car, a maroon Grand Prix. I don't know why we didn't take his Trans-AM. He's nodding at one of his co-workers, a pudgy, balding computer engineer dressed in a black pearly-button shirt and Levi's. *We have to appreciate every moment, Gene,* the man advises, touching my father's arm.

Brilliant philosophy, I sneer to myself, rolling my eyes.

"You're such a strong girl," Louise gushes, manhandling me into another hug. Her lips brush my cheek, leaving behind a pink scar. What she means is, she's impressed that I haven't cried—not at mass, not at the burial. A few of Mom's friends have commended me for this: *You're so strong. Your mother would be proud.* I want to scream, *Fucking clueless!* but I cannot make a sound. My throat, dry as the sun-drenched palms, swelled closed that morning. I am not brave. I am a coward. I can't speak. Would Mom be proud of that?

Nanny holds open the car door so that I can escape Louise's good intentions. Heat pours out of the back seat like a blast furnace, but I don't care. I lay back, willing the warmth to burn away my skin and bones, leaving nothing behind. I don't want to die so much as disappear.

"Gene, turn on the car," Nanny barks at Dad. It takes several minutes for him to end his conversation. I lay across the polyester fabric seat. By the time we finally drive away, abandoning my mother's body in the cemetery, my fever has hit. When we get home, Nanny puts me to bed with a temperature edging past 102. As I drift off to sleep, I hear the adults on the other side of my bedroom wall, gathered in our living room.

A lovely woman.

A shame.

They mutter the thinnest truths of praise with marbles in their mouths. I'm glad I don't have to watch them slurp weak Folger's from my mother's good china, which we never used.

That morning before my mother's funeral, I crept outside to study the brittle, alien snowflakes that had collected in our yard overnight. An inexplicable curtain of white had fallen into the shrugging shoulders of our saguaro cactus. Chalky drifts had gathered in the tiny cups of sage-green mesquite leaves—silent, and unnatural. My mother would have blanched to know that strangers had seen her body so unkempt when she died, the thick black leg hairs pushing up from her icy, dry skin like prickly pear cactus needles poking up through the snow.

Sometimes, when I miss her, I Google, *Snow in Phoenix, AZ.* The date comes up as proof of what is otherwise my strange fantasy: December 22, 1990, measurable snowfall, temperatures between 35 and 40 degrees. The snow was real, but the heat that I felt at my mother's funeral was all in my head—a product of the flu that kept me bed-ridden through Christmas that year.

I suppose I've never fully shaken that fever. Even today, twenty-eight years later, I keep expecting to snap out of it—to find that *this* life without her is the dream rather than the other way around. A sensuous parallel course in which I make better life choices for having my mother in it.

As my forty-fifth birthday approaches, the age at which my mother died, I realize how young she was. Now, I feel the weight of the living she missed, more than my childish loss of her. Despite my wish in the back seat of her car, it turns out that I *don't* want to disappear, after all. That's the trick of youth: the illusion of indestructibility outweighs the demonic attraction we have with ending our lives—and the gladness we feel for surviving.

How silently, and preternaturally swiftly, I watch time wend towards that inevitable conclusion, hastened by the foolish wish of a girl in crisis, unable to see in her grief that it will come true anyway.

poem

Stockholm Syndrome

katherine robbins

I can remember a time when your lips
smelled of formaldehyde,
and the cold that once drove me away,
is now keeping me close to your skin.

fiction

A Woman's Prerogative
josé enrique medina

In the future, when a man fucks up, when he commits an error that assaults the sensibility of his partner, the woman has the prerogative to push the button located on the back of his neck right above the atlas bone, which erases all memory of the offending incident from the man's mind, and she can force him to reenact the same scene, to make him go through the same paces, until he is able to navigate the labyrinth of choices in such a way that his performance satisfies her and his behavior no longer scratches her heart like a rusted hook.

Let's examine the famous case of Martín Herrera.[1]

One sunny afternoon, his memory is wiped clean. He finds himself standing on the northern corner of Cinco Puntos, an intersection of five streets in East Los Angeles. That crossing, which has five points like a star, is perhaps a labyrinth itself.

Intuition, or perhaps that homing device that urges birds to fly south for the winter, tells the man to cross the street and head south.

Once his shoes are planted on the sidewalk on the other side of the street, he looks both ways, seeing only empty lots with horns of broken glass returning glints of sun. With no structure around him, Martín asks himself, *Why did I cross the street?*

Suddenly, in front of him, an eight-story building appears. The fresh stucco and the smell of paint suggest that it's of new construction. Martín also realizes that the building did not materialize out of thin air, but that it was, in fact, always in front of him. He had simply overlooked the obvious.[2] This gives him a sense of déjà-vu, as if his life were an endless ring in which, at certain critical and inopportune moments, he overlooks the obvious. He also gets a vague presentiment that these oversights, however innocent on his behalf, are, to a large extent, going to add inches of sadness to his destiny.

He remembers his girlfriend lives in this condominium complex and pulls from his pocket the key she gave him. He opens the door, steps inside and faces a double staircase. The balustrades are painted white. Each landing branches off into another double staircase, and so on, into infinity. Intuitively, instantly, without having to put it in words, Martín understands that the forking staircases are a symbol for the way in which his own decisions divide

---

[1] Not to be confused with Martín Fierro, the protagonist of Jorge Luis Borges, that badminton enthusiast, builder of labyrinths and part-time occultist.

[2] Researchers at UC Irvine, headed by the cantankerous behaviorist Mary-Jane Holmes, perhaps with a wistful wink at the past, if not with a haughty snub at competing psychoanalytic practitioners, refer to these phenomena (objects marvelously reappearing after being grossly overlooked by men) as "modern-day magic."

into innumerable labyrinths.

He climbs the stairs, stops, and sits on the first landing.

A key clicks in the deadbolt, twisting the thumbturn.

When Martín hears this sound, two things happen at the same time.

His girlfriend Marta, who is home earlier than expected, walks in, and, a blonde appears seated next to him on the stair landing. This is another example of modern-day magic. She's wearing a see-through blouse and smiles. He is not surprised by the sudden appearance of the woman with golden hair because, like most men, he doesn't realize what he is doing until after he is caught.

In fairness to Martín, however, the narrator must point out that, by being with another woman, he is not doing anything wrong, because he and Marta are on an official break from each other. So "technically" Martín does not have anything to worry about, but the quotation marks around the word *technically* do not give him much confidence.

Another consideration that crosses his mind is that bringing his new "friend" to his on-hold girlfriend's house was not the best move.

Martín tells the blonde, "Go up to my room."

"No quiero drama," she says.

He brushes her away with a hand. "Go."

She stands and jogs up the stairs.

Unfortunately, she doesn't climb fast enough.

Marta, who is pushing a baby stroller full of shopping bags into the foyer, sees the bouncing mane of golden curls and says, "Oh hell no."

The next thing Martín considers is the race of the two women. Marta is biracial—Mexican mother, black father.[3] Her kinky hair is pulled back, twisted into a small tight ball, and reprimanded with a pomade. The shiny grease succeeds in straightening her hair, but even so, ancestry fights against the straightening magic of the oil, retaining a wavy rhythm.[4] Although she has yellow hair and blue eyes, Martín believes his visitor, born in Bolivia, is not Caucasian. On a job application, she would check the box next to Latino/Hispanic, not White/Caucasian. He thinks the Spanish language and Latino culture overwrite white genes, creating a special Latin race, combining the best attributes of the white race and the Hispanic culture. For Martín, a light-skinned Mexican, nothing can override black genes. The mark of that disgrace shows through any mask of culture.[5]

Given the snubs Marta has heard against her dark skin, Martín is sure that bringing a "white" woman, not just any other woman, to her home

---

[3] When a black man dates a white woman, he is said to be "upgrading" to the lighter races. If a white woman couples with a black man, she is diagnosed with "jungle fever," a type of illness and not too-subtle suggestion that black men look like gorillas.

[4] If you were to inspect her head closely, it would resemble a surface of water rippled by a breeze.

[5] When Martín was five years old, he heard his aunts make these comments about babies: "As long as my niece is able to get pregnant, who cares if the baby comes out dark," "He's so fair-skinned. How cute!" and "Poor thing, she was born dark." The Mexican women loaded these prejudices into the child's mind like bullets into a gun.

adds alcohol to Marta's wound. To soften Marta's pain and to take part of the blame off his shoulders, Martín would like to explain to her that technically—again that word—his companion is not white. Even though for the most part the nature of women is a mystery to him, he understands enough to know that splitting hairs in this case would result in a more explosive situation. So, against his natural masculine inclination to set the record straight and to speak objectively without regard to emotional implications, he decides to keep his mouth shut on this subject.

He is lucky in another respect: Marta is a classy woman and won't make a scene about having another woman in her home.

Two girls enter behind Marta. This perhaps further explains Marta's impressive self-constraint: she does not want to fight in front of others. The two girls are tall, thin, fifteen years old. They have shocks of loose frizzy hair. The backlight from the open door throws into relief the curl in it and emphasizes its dark color, which to Martín makes them look more African than Marta. *Are they Marta's sisters?* he asks himself.[6] He guesses that, because the girls are darker than Marta, they are probably only half-sisters—i.e., her black father impregnated a black woman.

The girls look at Martín standing at the top of the stairs, at Marta and then at each other. The way in which the three women inhale and straighten their shoulders gives Martín the uncomfortable sensation that all this has happened before, maybe countless times. He feels disconnected from them, alone, like an actor in the wings, waiting for someone to invite him onstage.

"Grab your things and go up to your rooms," Marta tells the girls.

Although they look like twins, one girl is darker and shorter.

The lighter girl whispers to Marta, "He looks sick. Should we help him?"

"He doesn't do shit for us," the darker one replies.

"Girls. Now. Upstairs," commands Marta.

The light girl lifts her bags from the stroller, darts one last long look up at Martín, as if through her glance she would like to impart the information he so desperately needs, and which she desperately wants him to have.

The dark girl frowns.

"Maybe this time," the light girl says, squeezing Marta's hand.

The girls climb a staircase, opposite to the one on which Martín stands, and enter their bedrooms.

"Who are those girls?" Martín asks Marta.

"Your daughters."

"How can I have black daughters?"

"Not again, Martín. Please—look at the stroller."

He looks at his white arms. "How could I have black daughters?"

She pushes the stroller towards him. "Look at the stroller."

He keeps staring at his skin. "I don't understand."

---

[6] The attentive reader will recall that Martín recently underwent a memory-erasing process. Forgetting who people are, however, is not a part of the procedure. This negative side-effect (excessive memory loss) is often seen in subjects who undergo too many mind wipes. It may also, however, be due to selective remembering (i.e., Martín wants to forget who these girls are).

"I can't do this again, Martín."

Marta runs up the stairs and slams her bedroom door.

Standing all alone, Martín looks down at the stroller abandoned in the vestibule, tires corroded and scuffed, black handles worn to gray by years of use.

Suddenly, like a camera's aperture blades swooshing together and forming a full circle, all of Martín's memories swirl together and form a complete picture. He remembers everything.[7]

His shoulders relax, he can breathe again.

It's true, he thinks. Those girls are my daughters. I haven't spent time with them in ages.

I've been fucking up and reliving the same moment, again and again, for thirteen years.

Each time I get to this point, I'm given four choices. But I always pick the wrong one. Because of that, they erase my memory, place me on the northern corner of the Cinco Puntos intersection, and I have to navigate through my maze of choices all over again.

Marta's up in her bedroom, waiting for me to finally make the right decision.

I don't want to reenact the same thing forever.

This time, I'm going to choose wisely, so that I don't hurt Marta. Besides, there are only four options in this puzzle. How can I get lost inside a labyrinth with only four points?[8]

My four choices to fix the mess I created are:

Option number one: run immediately to Marta's bedroom, get on knees and ask for forgiveness.

That's what I should do. Wait! Take your time, consider all the options and consequences. Maybe that's the mistake I've made in the past, acting too quickly. Reacting out of animal impulse instead of tranquilly thinking about all my choices.

Besides, after thirteen years of waiting, Marta ought to be tired of me and my inability to do shit right. I can't imagine a sweet reception in her bedroom. She must be up there right now, pacing back and forth, praying to get

---

[7] The stroller is the object* that triggered his memory recall. He remembers that that's the reason why Marta pushes it every day.

* Inventor of the memory-erasing procedure, Nancy Lynée Woo testified in Congress that she based the object-trigger technology on 17th century magic, specifically the Medal of Saint Benedict. "That talisman," she said, "was used in 1647 witchcraft trials to torture women and to exorcise them of independence and free thought. I find it just and necessary to take a similar object-based approach to science, but in a more humane way, to give men another chance to correct their aberrant behavior and to improve the relations between the sexes.

"The object makes men recall they are facing a multiple-choice test. They also remember the number and nature of the choices available to them. Under no circumstances, however, will they recall their prior wrong responses because that would: 1) make it too easy for them to solve the puzzle of their own behavior and 2) not lead to true change of the heart."

[8] Apparently, our hero did not read "The Garden of Forking Paths," in which the protagonist gets lost in an infinite labyrinth constructed of only two points.

rid of me. No, no, the correct answer is option number two.

Option number two: run immediately to Vanessa's bedroom, the light daughter, grab her hand and ask her to beg her mother on my behalf to forgive me.

Yes, why wasn't that my first thought? Since she was little, she was my favorite daughter. I caressed and spoiled her like no other woman. She is my strongest ally. The two of us, like two battering rams, could knock down the iron door of Marta's heart. It's the easiest thing to do in the world.

He makes to run to Vanessa's bedroom, but then he stops.

Wait, wait, he thinks. I told myself I was going to consider my options before acting. And look at me, I don't have a pinch of patience. I can't even do the things I say I'm going to do. No wonder Marta hates me. I'm a beast of passion, without an inch of reason.

And, now that I think about it, running to Vanessa is too easy, a sign I'm a coward. I should do the difficult thing. And that's option number three.

Option number three: run immediately to Nessi's bedroom, the dark daughter, hang my head and ask her to forgive me.

What better way to impress Marta than to ask forgiveness from her little monster? Besides, asking Nessi for forgiveness doesn't have to be difficult. Because I didn't do anything wrong,[9] my apology doesn't have to be sincere. The important thing is to squash Marta's false perceptions that I treated her dark daughter worse than her lighter-skinned daughter. Once Marta sees what a great man I am, that I'm capable of admitting when I'm wrong, she will have no other choice than to run to my arms, hug me and tell me I'm a good man.[10]

---

[9] A third example of modern-day magic. In addition to making buildings and people reappear, magical thinking can make actions disappear. "I didn't do anything wrong" refers to, among other things, denying he was the father of the two girls. A white-skinned Latino, he got scared upon seeing that the new-born girls were much darker, not whiter, than the mother. During the pregnancy, he fantasized about the whitening effect his skin would have on Marta's offspring. Only after the results of a secret paternity test, which confirmed his fatherhood and the treacherous nature of genes, did he step up to the role of provider. However, using magical thinking, he forgot the paternity test results, continued blaming the darker child for Marta's imagined infidelity, and poured love on the lighter child. To ease his conscience, he told himself he invested more time in the white girl, not because she was white, but because she was larger and healthier looking. When the point of guilt popped through that layer of logic, he changed the scenario, asking himself, What would you do if the white child was the smaller one? In that case, he would take more care of the white child, not because she was white, but because black-skinned children are stronger and do not need much help. In this way, like the shoulder strap of a seatbelt that self-adjusts to allow one's chest to move while tying one in place, his logic both accommodated itself to obtain the result he wanted no matter the situation, and locked him into his prejudices.

[10] The narrator, the product of a biracial union (Chinese mother, black father), often called "Chinig" (Chinese + nigger) in college and having a morsel of experience in these situations, would like to propose to academia a new term to describe this type of racism which refuses detection in the mind of its propagators and which allows them to see themselves as "good people" and which is capable of circumventing whatever logic or kindness you throw at it: self-adjusting racism.

In a story about the difficulties of the two sexes understanding each other, it's imperative

He takes a step towards Nessi's bedroom.

Did God not give me a brain? he asks himself, stopping. Or am I cursed to be an octopus of impulses, tying my arms around the option closest to me, without contemplating all the possibilities? That is my fatal flaw, acting without thinking.

I should pick number four.

Option number four: run immediately to my bedroom and ask the blonde to get the hell out of here.

How clear it is! I have this bitch here fucking over the three women in my life. I should charge into my room, grab her by the hair and drag her out of this house. Yes, and the noisier the better, so that my three loves in their rooms hear how much I respect them, how much I want to repair the damage I did.

He turns and starts up the stairs towards his bedroom.

Do you realize what you just did? he asks himself, stopping. You just gave your back to your woman. You did the biggest mistake in a woman's eyes: you put another woman in front of her. Always, always, always, you have to put your lady first. Now I know, one hundred percent, the best choice is option number one.

He descends the stairs and pauses on the landing.

But to be sure I'm making the best decision, he says to himself, let me go over all my options just one more time …

Like she has done every day for the past thirteen years, Marta waits in her bedroom. She wrings her hands, adjusts and readjusts a black-and-white photo of her and Martín on her dresser. Since all the paths in the labyrinth lead to her bedroom door, she doesn't care which option he picks. She just wants him to choose.

After one hour, she realizes, once again, he has gotten lost in the corridors of doubt.

She silently turns the knob of her bedroom door, walks behind Martín, pulls down the collar of his printed shirt, presses the button behind his head with an emphatic thumb, and forces him to start all over again.

---

to raise the question of racism and the effect race has in the interactions we have with each other. I would like to separate the two (sex and race), but it's impossible. Something that makes me lose faith, because, in effect, we are inside a labyrinth inside another labyrinth.

nonfiction

Through Our Soil

deanna hershiser

"Though the problems of the world are increasingly complex,
the solutions remain embarrassingly simple."

Bill Mollison, known as the father of permaculture ("permanent agriculture")

First, I notice pizza boxes. My son, James, has flattened and laid them across grass and weeds in our garden area, the small rectangle where we failed this past spring even to plant corn and beans, where October brambles compete with red potatoes. Before work, James is out there with cardboard, digging some, sprinkling leaves, and setting into the ground a few unfamiliar plantstarts. I shake my head, wondering what his dad will think. Mostly, with cautious optimism, I am intrigued.

Something about dirt beneath his fingernails and a fresh whiff of—licorice?—as James steps inside to don his bike helmet lightens my spirit.

When our kids were little, Tim and I signed papers, closing the deal on four bedrooms, attached garage, one and a quarter baths. Our suburban home same age as Tim had been brought into being, like my husband, in the Willamette Valley. Long before Tim or our house existed, my father picked beans during summers at the farm this lot belonged to.

By the time Tim and I bought our place, the surrounding neighborhood's lawn-quilt featured mature crimson maples, cherry blossoms, dogwoods, tall cedars behind our back fence, and the random sequoia. In our yard, a rhododendron and sword fern got too much sun in front, a peony sputtered blossoms near the T-post clothesline out back, and peace roses glowed on the garage's south side.

Soon Tim brought home a satellite dish. It was one of those immense, free-standing black orbs like you see next to TV stations. Tim worked for a TV station, and this dish had been decommissioned. From the center of its mesh "petals" an electronic stamen aimed heavenward. James, not yet two, clutched his soft blanket and watched Daddy dig. Into the deep hole in the lawn, Tim poured cement for the dish's trunk-like support.

Seasons swelled past us after that, buffeting our structures, wafting leaf breezes and acrid tomato scents over the back step. Sometimes I paused before taking out the recycling to breathe a bit. Late springtime, James and neighbor children chirped an imagined, epic Super Mario story across mossy grass while lawnmowers from adjoining yards bellowed in differing keys. Tim busied himself building a shed for his mower. There, he also housed the bike he rode to work and a chainsaw for logs he emptied onto the driveway, cut, and stacked near the rosebush, burning seasoned pieces in our woodstove all winter.

The April after James's first creative layering of pizza boxes and leaves, I wander out back. The licorice scent I noticed last fall exudes from a soft green filigree James will later tell me is fennel. Near the house something blossoms—its deep pink, hanging flowers are attracting hummingbirds. I don't know it yet, but I'm destined to welcome this dainty flowering currant each successive spring with joy.

On the north side are plants I do know: male and female kiwis flank the clothesline; nearby is a grape cutting from a friend. James planted the grape next to the old, now dormant satellite dish; it climbs the orb apace.

Stepping back, I marvel. This leafy business unfurls greatly. Will we become an orchard? A jungle? I don't quite understand what is happening to our yard.

From childhood, James was a guy who wanted to understand. Before age 10, he learned the Fujita scale for measuring tornado severity, and he memorized numbers between a billion and a decillion. This before Google existed. He studied clouds, weather patterns, maps, and mountains. When we took him hiking, James taught me the names of Oregon peaks besides Mt. Hood: Jefferson, the Three Sisters, Diamond Peak, and more.

Then came darker seasons. As an older teen, James kept to his room, his Gameboy gathering dust, his hiking books and maps an unkempt pile. He spent time online and filling spiral-bound notebooks. Nights were emotional minefields. He grew thinner, his glance toward me anxious. Tim and I sought help, and a kind counselor listened to our son. No magic cure existed. At home, Tim and I stepped with extra care, like cloud-tenders, through the hallway.

Looking back, I'm sure I could have done things differently. No junk food? Locked computer, discouraging study? Friends turned away whose ideas differed from ours? Maybe sanitizing air, water, and all beasts of the field … parental second guesses must number in the decillions.

Suburbia's continuing chorus—traffic and groceries and classes past the crosswalk—kept its pace as the Earth made signs of turning. My stomach knots loosened the day James, by now a high school graduate, mentioned he had noticed a mom and pop plant nursery just down River Road. He asked for a ride to check it out.

Around midsummer, city workers enter our back yard and chainsaw two rogue maples: leafy, teenaged jokesters who've grown into the power lines. I grieve their loss but attempt to see the consolation in this season of more and more plantings by James. With the city's coupon for replacement shrubs in hand, he and Tim shop a store called Down to Earth and find three varieties of blueberry bushes. James then plants them beneath the satellite dish/grape arbor.

Tim, I can see, takes the expanding garden in stride, and yet I sense my husband's tension. He doesn't know anymore where to mow in the backyard. Mint is growing by the deck, as well as a patch of sage. The front driveway, too, has become lined with seedlings. Such changes may bring all kinds of extra work after James moves out.

One August evening, I trail my barefoot son as he waters new plants. I'm asking questions. So that one, over by the deck, will become a fig tree? Huh. How about that bush near the strawberries? Oh, right. You told me: seaberry, or sea buckthorn. Hm. And this? Black currant, okay. Over here, milkweed. You're sure it'll attract monarch butterflies? Wow.

James enrolls in a fall class for certification in permaculture design. Attending his end of term presentation with other students' families, I cajole my brain to concentrate, to retain at least some information.

When learning permaculture design methods, the students explain, a starting point is noticing watersheds. Discovering the land's features, even in urban spaces, gives clues about where to plant things.

I'm wandering in thought to our back shed, picturing a fountain gushing from it. No, I remember. James told me he watches for ground slopes, for where the water *sheds*.

Then there are plant choices, the students say: those that benefit many pollinators (not just honeybees) will help save insects that give us fruit and berries, plus food for grazing animals. I know James has rescued plants near highway 99 before city mowers could reach them. Comfry, lupin, camas, and more. So some weeds *are* critical.

One student stresses the fact that turning one's yard into a "food forest" actually makes growing things easier over time. Perennials return each year, she says. Borage and beneficial grasses reseed themselves and often are drought resistant.

Nice, those words. A chorus of hope. Sounds like Tim and I can't easily destroy what James has labored so hard to begin.

Perhaps permaculture's main importance, the students go on, is the restorative building of soil. Pizza boxes and leaves, I'm thinking. But they explain the process is wholistic, more than the sum of its pieces. When people start designing agriculture to restore, rather than decimate, topsoil, more places on Earth can feed us, feed our grandchildren, feed those nations desolated by drought-inducing neglect.

Seven years after James first studied permaculture, I pause on the back step before sunset, taking pictures. Another winter has ended; I'm encouraged to see a bumblebee aiming past me toward a thimbleberry blossom. The sage is softer, greening. Earlier, James rode over briefly from his apartment downtown.

Our backyard's lawn has dwindled to a mown path winding between trees, shrubs and structures, the native patches, and new finds James brings in. Every spring and summer we eat homegrown artichokes, honey berries, mulberries, Asian pears, apples, noninvasive blackberries, aronia berries, currants, cherries, milkthistle seeds, two fig varieties, and more.

James continues working his day job while on the side tutoring people about plants, helping many build soil in their yards and reap the healing benefits.

On the back step I muse, glancing over where summer grapevines will reach into apple branches and kiwi vines will twirl across the old clothesline. Lacy lomatiums will bloom and send roots deep into soil.

A while ago, James shared with me about coming through the anxious episodes in his teens. He said one day he recognized that growing things were like mountains, only closer—like numbers, only tangible. He could go to them, touch them, inhale them anytime. They would receive his care, and they would care for him.

For all this, for the plants, I have become grateful. Evening shadow-lights beckon in the yard, and I push off the step amid scents of mint and licorice.

poem

The Burden of Fruit

cathleen calbert

There's the apple and our first foreclosure,
the pomegranate and never getting to be a girl
again once encumbered by the hell of love,

the peaches I dare not eat in the street
with my bee-stung lips and baby grays,
so-called mutton dressed as lamb as I am,

(Is the Mock Orange truly
worse than real groves that say
sun's fine and love lasts?)

the blackberry, blackberry, blackberry
addiction of poetry, God help all of us scribblers.
Sure, but I mean something more mundane:

after stroking, smelling, and knocking
away in the produce section of Stop 'n Slop,
I bite into tartness, mush, or dry string at home.

(Bananas, pure as yogurt,
soon lead to darker visions
of sugar and flour.)

Thus, I plunge into the usual despair:
how sad it is, how unfair and disheartening.
I remember the hope and care I took:

I saw, I chose, I bought.
This was to be the beginning of everything:
a new future, a beautiful attitude.

(Who'd take the goodness
of grapes and shrink desire
into duty's grim raisin?)

Clean-living folks own fruit.
They place it on crumb-free countertops
for a nutritious snack after sex or tennis.

Fruit-eaters don't need wine to sleep.
They don't wonder over the meaning
of existence after naps.

(Lawrence's poem made me
want to eat figs and stop
sleeping with men.)

I buy fruit but live in fear:
what if it's bruises and rotten softness again,
an underbelly of white mold in the morning?

The moment of ripeness is as brief as a man's love
when that man sleeps on the couch or, when awake,
eats only cheese. Clearly, he's no help to me.

(He squeezed his half
of the juicy grapefruit into a slit
and dubbed it "Cunty Face.")

Fruit glowers in my cobalt bowl.
Promise and beauty shade into something
more menacing like a woman in her forties.

Good strawberry, tender plum:
your bounty is my burden.
How shall I swallow all of you in time?

Jack, a Kind of First
peter clarke

Jack's dad promised enough wedding money to creep out Jesus. How much could an auto mechanic care about his transgender daughter's marriage to a singer on food stamps? Enough to make that pot belly of his suck in until he birthed five paychecks, I guess.

But then he caught wind of my excitement. Just like that, he wanted to back out like the jerk I figured he was from the start.

"Let it go," said Jack, her pretty face sad with terrible makeup. I could sense her frustration with my over-eagerness.

"Could, but not gonna," I said.

"I don't want him there anyway. He'll ruin it."

"I love me some ruined things."

"You know there are different classes of ruined things. This is a ruined thing like food you can't eat. It's no good."

"But ruined food, you just puke it up!"

"I hate puking."

"No way! When was the last time you puked? It's like primo catharsis. Especially if you really might die if you don't. One second you're poisoned to death for sure, then you're retching your guts out all over the place in a spontaneous letting go as intense as gravity calling it quits, or whatever. Then suddenly you feel like a million bucks."

"Well, there is the money ..."

"It's worth a frickin' shot, babe."

The second you see yourself having troubles with love, you know you can't go away emptyhanded. Love in the normal sense requires giving. But in times of crisis, it's time to take! Just like lawyers live and breathe this, I've been training.

Jack tried playing in my band but that didn't work out. Then she showed up at a Wiccan full moon dance and we drank wine out of the same gourd. It spilled all over her shirt and her new implants looked stellar. Next day she was at a coffee shop hung over and I asked if she'd marry me.

"Dad's still paying off my surgeries and I haven't told him the details. He thinks it was knee surgery."

"Don't you know who I am?"

"Sure. I tried out for your band, remember?"

"Dude, I mean, don't you know what I do?"

"No."

"Okay, I'm the guy who gets married once a year—trying to break the world record for marriages and all that shit. They wrote about it in the paper and a few lawsuits make it extra culturally relevant. I'm kind of a big deal when it comes to the marriage biz."

She gave me queer looks. Gave me that scowl with the "aw, come on" eyes.

"I mean, fuck your dad," I said. "Getting married is a huge sham!"

"Sounds like with you it is."

"Totally the opposite. With me it's the greatest. It's a blast. I'm the only thing happening in modern relationships today."

"So why me?"

"It's not everyone who drinks wine from gourds."

"Ever married a trans chick before?"

"Transvestite once."

"How'd that go?"

"Same as all the others."

"Good?"

"Humans are the best! Don't you just want to marry all of them?"

"Even that guy?"

Some cranky bastard a few tables away. Dressed in the shambles of normcore. Sitting at his computer Googling "rocks" with a clear hard on.

"Hell yeah!" I said.

"Don't."

I went over to the guy. Leaned on his table.

"You like rocks?" I asked.

"Yes," he answered, smug as hell.

"God, me too. Want to get married?"

Slowly dying with cancer in a hospital but at least you've got the nursing staff. All your guts in the street after a car crash but look at all the party lights of everyone coming to the rescue. Silently, at night, going with your arms wrapped around your younger wife, fast asleep. What are people even thinking when they promise love eternal? Shot in an alley by a chump on crack and you just wish he'd got your head and not your damn groin.

Doing this thing right means all the full ceremony my backyard just can't offer. Melissa had to wear a plastic wedding gown as a last-minute invention. Sarah had to settle for a plain chocolate box cake instead of her dream of marijuana brownies for everyone. She also wanted more of a wedding bed than my blow-up mattress.

"Hey girl," I said, "It's no crime being poor! It just sucks but we'll get by!"

She got pregnant by some other prick while we were still married just to hurt me. I saved up, talked my dealer down, and sent weed brownies to the baby shower.

With Jack: we picked a date and settled on the park by the water. Had some elaborate schemes for catering and entertainment. Began to research all the best wedding rituals dreamed up by pagan cultures. Jack talked up her

Wiccan buddies for ideas. We made certain the stars were properly aligned for the next full moon.

"Shouldn't we wait till our wedding night?" Jack asked, face down on my bed.

"That goes against my only true virtue: not procrastinating."

"But just in this case—for the full moon, ya know?"

"You're shy!"

"No!"

"Damn, you are! I knew it! Come on, take your panties off."

"I hate that word!"

"What, panties? Panties, panties, panties!"

She ran up against the wall, looking around for something to bash me with.

"It has nothing to do with the wedding ..." I said, crazy soft when she expected screams.

"What do you mean?"

"If we just do it after the wedding, then it's just another part of the stupid-ass ceremony I want to destroy anyway."

"Just not right now, okay?"

"Ah, come on," I pressed against her, but she slipped loose, grabbing her bag, ready to walk out.

"It's okay for me to say no."

"I can say no, too, and see how you like it."

"Oh yeah?"

"No, no, no."

She came back the next night. Immediately asked for a beer and asked what I was up to.

"Right now? Researching some fine points for my lawsuits. Pretty exhilarating and shit. Legal system's fucked up."

"Okay, well let's make a deal."

"Sure."

"Let me in your band and we can do it."

I stood up. Had a sip of beer. Thought it over.

"And you'll let me say panties?"

"No, that's going too far. But you can take them off."

"Okay, you got it, babe. It's a deal."

Played a knockout show a few weeks later and introduced our new bassist as my future wife. All my ex-wives in the crowd went nuts like a real bunch of groupies.

First thing, if you ever want to set the record for the world's most marriages, definitely start a rock band. Then marry a band manager. Then a booking agent. Then a chick to make your bros jealous while you get your glam shots and album covers made.

Then marry all your fans so at least you'll have people to add to your guest list when you've been on tour for five years and your tunes still blow.

Check, check, and check.

Sometime along the line, might as well marry a bassist while you're at it.

No one gets society. The core of it is purely primordial for one thing. The rest of it is either random or based on somebody else's vision of an ideal. All of it is off its nuts and basically just about sex and trying for all it's worth to keep this marriage thing working. Everyone's walking around thinking, "How can we protect this marriage thing at all costs?" Great question!

That's when Jack's dad wavered. Seems he looked me up. Could just picture the expression on his face—I looked him up, too—when he read about my lawsuits in the news. "Serial marrier makes mockery of traditional values. Hide your daughters!"

He wanted to know what the hell he was paying for if this thing wasn't going to be forever.

"Let's go talk to him."

Jack was worried. "What would you say?"

"Nothin'. He'd just see I'm a nice, kindhearted kid, ya feel?"

"He liked guys with …"

"What, trust funds?"

"Family values."

"Oh wow. Okay, you're right, I might be out of luck with that. I don't even know where you get those."

How do you unlock the key to a mechanic's heart? You take your car in for a tune up, duh!

Good thing my sweet ride's got hella complex issues. You could diagnose the shit out of it and still find bugs in its engine pipes, dry-rot in the carburetor for days.

It was the earliest I'd gotten up in a decade and my nice kid face was struggling. But what's a mechanic, after all, if not another fellow human needing love?

"It's a real pleasure, Mr. Fry," I said almost genuinely when we met at the auto shop.

He eyed me like some kind of tax collector but shook my hand. I could tell he wanted to ignore that this was happening and get right on with the day's grease and gaskets.

"I'm Lucian," I said. "Friend of Jack's."

"When I heard Jack was getting married …"

He was all worked up. Couldn't express himself except to get red in the face. A man of few words! I shuffled my feet and waited for him to continue. I waited as long as possible.

"But anyway," I said finally, "my car here, it's got some noise it's making, plus it just hardly gets started and barely goes anymore. Think it's the brakes?

The accelerator …?"

That's all it took to get him back in action. Dude's alright. He said a few things in mechanic speak and we were back in business. The trusty commerce game. In this together, we both stood there trying to wrap our brains around the issues of this rusty old junkheap.

Everything fell into place. The stars, the moon, even the money. We had enough alright. More than I'd ever seen in one place, for sure.

"Nervous, babe?"

"No."

"Is that a sad no or a shy no?"

"I don't know."

We were standing in a large circle of friends, ex-wives, and Wiccans. The full moon was out like a sterile, loving hospital light.

"Your pop's here in spirit."

"He disowned me."

"Don't say that!"

"He did."

"The surgeries?"

"No. I told him about my surgeries. He didn't …"

"So, it was the wedding?"

"Yes."

"Oh … figured that might happen, when he wouldn't pay for it."

"Didn't he?"

"Sold my car. It wasn't worth a dime except for the stereo, which was frickin' priceless."

Jack teared up. My ex-wives took notice and teared up, too. The Wiccans played along and began to wail and sob, tossing back swigs of wine by the gourd-full. In the center of this hot-blooded frenzy, we carried out our pagan rituals in silence.

Woke up in the woods in the early dawn with a Wiccan on either side. That's the great thing about being intoxicated. You can just say fuck it. I shivered and pulled the Wiccans closer.

"Jack's gone!" said a panicked voice in the back of my mind.

"Big deal," shrugged the rest of me. "Check out all my Wiccan palls, still good practically naked girls if ever I've seen any."

That was the party of parties, alright. People would be talking about the horrors and elations of that wedding day for years to come. Only I wouldn't know how Jack felt about it. I knew she wouldn't show up to the courthouse later, wouldn't sign the papers, wouldn't make it official. In the eyes of the law, we wouldn't be married. But at least the Wiccans would count it. Wouldn't they?

"Jack!" I yelled in my half-asleep mind. "What do you say, Jack? Does it count?"

Octavio Paz Addresses Marie-José

anthony seidman

Do not move; unbutton your blouse, let fall
your skirt which is wheat the wind combs; that
is our world.

I have choked on politics, watched
money rasp as ashes rising up chimneys, and sat
in the white atrium of silence.

Do not speak; undo your hair, let fall
your dress which is water tempting the moon; that
is our parliament.

Calendar has turned full
circle, fusing the deities of water, smoke.
I am with you as a draft of syllables,
an echo that knocks, fades, and I am
indifferent to the dying world because here
I sleep without you.

Without you, dark orchard,
tree of my blood, blade of noon.
Two birds took flight in your eyes:
the one without wings, the other on fire.

Malama Honolua

beau ewan

There's not much of a beach at Honolua Bay. The sand isn't flaky white like it is back on the East Coast. Out here on Maui, somewhere near the middle of the Pacific Ring of Fire, the sand is sparse, coarse, and hiding in between the volcanic crags of coral covering the shoreline. Forget umbrellas, beach chairs, and sand castles. Forget finding a spot for the towel. Simply walking across this beach is difficult. I'm jumping from boulder to boulder with my surfboard tucked under one arm, teetering and stumbling over each wobbly stone. There's some rhythm in the ocean that I can never find back on shore, especially this morning, with my legs still shaking after riding waves that broke for nearly a quarter of a mile.

Since I began teaching in Maui, almost two years ago, I haven't been late to work once. But this morning, after taking advantage of an unseasonably late northeast ground swell—I paddled out just before sunrise hoping to surf the bay alone—I'm cutting it close. I have no time for slipping or falling on these rocks, so I slow down to move faster, and make every step count. At the end of the beach, Lipoa Point, I begin the climb up towards my truck. There's a natural trail carved by runoff during the rainy season, the result of which is a series of sketchy switchbacks that snake up a bluff. I say my Aloha to passing surfers heading the opposite way, all of us slipping along the sloping trail, searching for footholds in the folding jungle walls. Near the top, on the edge of the red clay parking lot, I run into Les Potts, an older surfer and a fellow haole. That word, haole, is island slang for white people. Potts looks up at me as he's planting a hand-carved sign into the soil: *Malama Honolua*.

"Take care of the bay? Right?" I ask him.

"Believe me, bro," he says, "we're gonna need to."

I'm not quite sure what he means by this, so I just go about my routine and place my surfboard in the bed of my truck. I reach up into the wheel well where I stashed my keys and grab a dirty towel from the cab to cover me while I change out of my wet boardshorts and into my khakis. I sit on the truck's gate and tie my shoes when Potts slowly approaches. "How was the surf?" he asks.

Potts is in his sixties, probably less than six feet tall, and salty, with a tan complexion and leathery skin. He has gray shaggy hair and wears aviator sunglasses, though not funky or chic ones, but the understated and functional shades that my grandfather would have worn during his Air Force days. I don't know Potts personally, but I've heard about him and seen him chatting with some of the older crew in the parking lot.

"Incredible," I tell him, grinning. "I had it all to myself for a while."

I know from the coconut wireless that Potts has lived here forever, since the sixties, and that he plays music and shapes surfboards for a living. A neighbor of mine, Elie, belongs to a small cohort of haole surfers my age who were born on this island. He once showed me this psychedelic rock 'n' roll film shot in Maui called Rainbow Bridge, where a younger Potts is surfing to the music of Jimi Hendrix, who visited the Valley Isle in 1970.

"That role made Potts a legend here," Elie told me when we were watching the Youtube video on his laptop. Elie's parents also moved here in the late sixties, where they apparently remain kind of stuck. His folks live upcountry, on the slopes of Mount Haleakala, where they're part of a "shared agricultural project"—the coded job description for planters, harvesters, and distributors of Maui Wowie—not far from where the Hendrix concert was held. "It was a free show," he told me, "for this really heady meditation group that used to meet up there. The Rainbow Bridge Occult." Hendrix and Potts supposedly became close friends during the filming of Rainbow Bridge.

"You're a lucky man to surf the bay alone," Potts tells me. "Tough to avoid a crowd these days." He smiles pensively towards the group of surfers just starting down the trail, then to the end the parking lot, where several SUVs with piles of surfboards strapped to their roofs are pulling off of Highway 30.

Though we're only miles away from where kitschy resort signs guide Maui's tourist traffic, the highway up here is a feral road still roaming wild, with crushed palm fronds, splattered mangoes and squashed bougainvillea sprinkled over the pavement. Beyond here, there's not a single house, store, or hotel lobby for nearly an hour's drive. Not until the road circles back to the other side of the island, ending where it first began. But on mornings like this, in the red clay parking lot of Honolua Bay, stereos blast, truck doors slam, boards are waxed, and another dozen or so surfers are making their way down towards the waves.

"Have a good one," I tell Potts. I secure my surfboard with a bungee cord to keep it from uplifting in the passing trade winds.

Even though Potts is a noticeably quiet kind of guy, ever since I've watched Rainbow Bridge, it's impossible not to think of him as somebody with stories to tell. He moved to this outer island during the Vietnam War, long before Maui became what it is today—the premier vacation spot for wealthy Californians and honeymooners around the globe. I've heard that the locals hated white people so much back then, the airport terminal was tagged with graffiti that said *HAOLES GO HOME*. To a certain extent, this sentiment survives; it's not uncommon to see locals with bumper stickers that read *I GREW HERE, YOU FLEW HERE* or *NO HAWAIIAN, NO ALOHA*. Things were far worse, however, when Potts landed here. There were no hospitality jobs yet. No jobs outside of the sugar, pineapple, and coffee fields. Those like Potts who stayed regardless were not rebelliously protesting against American society as much as they were peacefully dropping out of it all together. They picked up surfboards instead of picket signs and slept in island jungles halfway between Vietnam and everything they had ever known.

As I'm turning to get out of the parking lot, I gesture a shaka towards Potts—the equivalent of a peace sign for surfers—and he throws one back at me. Then, he just stands there, alone, staring at the bay below.

Pulling out of the parking lot, I slam on the gas and speed down the highway, negotiating hairpin turns and boulders the size of bowling balls, which regularly fall onto the road up here. They remain wherever they land until the county decides it's time to remove them again. With my windows down, I can hear the dissonance created between my truck's engine and the off-key symphony of this untamed jungle, composed by the high-pitched croaks of coqui frogs, chirping myna birds, and banyan trees squeaking in the island breeze. When the highway climbs up the ridgeline into the resort town of Kapalua, I glance into the rearview to see massive waves breaking into the bay, with whitewater and a rising tide now working hand in hand to take back the boulder-laden beach. Before me, the landscape becomes groomed and irrigated, dotted with timeshares and mansions, fairways and putting greens.

On the mauka side of the road, towards the mountains, several gated communities emerge in the foothills and fallow pineapple fields. This entire area, from here to Honolua Bay and beyond, is owned by one of Hawaii's oldest and largest corporations, the Maui Land and Pineapple Company.

ML&P has its roots with the Baldwin family, a clan of New England missionaries who moved here in the 1800's, bringing both religion and smallpox to the Hawaiian people. The Baldwins treated the land as a massive agricultural commodity. Over the course of several decades, five major companies—commonly referred to as "The Big Five"—controlled all of Hawaii's agricultural economy: Castle and Cook, once known as the Dole Food Company; C. Brewer & Co, the world's largest producer of macadamia nuts; American Factors, a conglomerate specializing in retail, sugarcane, and land development; Theo H. Davies & Co, a former plantation company that owns fast food franchises in Hawaii along with Mercedes Benz and Jaguar dealerships; and Alexander & Baldwin, a corporation owned by the original Baldwin family, which continues to be one of Hawaii's largest landowners.

Before missionaries stole the land and started these massive corporations, the Hawaiians farmed using the ahupua'a system, which divided the land and all of its resources into plots extending from the mountains to the sea. Each division was adjusted as necessary to feed its surrounding population. While the ahupua'a system is seen as one of the most efficient examples of subsistence-based farming ever encountered by the West, if Maui were to be quarantined today—a possibility in the event of an avian flu outbreak—the entire island would run out of food in less than one week. Nearly every food item here is imported from the mainland. Even the few remaining sugar operations on Maui send their cane to the mainland for processing before it's shipped back here and sold on shelves as "Real Maui Sugar."

The mansions and hotels I'm speeding past are almost entirely new, most of them constructed when ML&P converted its many pineapple fields into real estate ventures during the 1990's. Any agricultural operations that survived into the new millennium were either condensed or eliminated altogether. Today, the word pineapple in ML&P just adds flavor to Hawaii's premiere real estate corporation, publicly traded on the New York Stock Exchange, with its largest stakeholder being Steve Case, founder of America Online.

I drive through the towns of Napili and Kahana and pass the entrance to Kaanapali, a hotel-lined beach with tiki bars, restaurants and hotel towers, before hitting the town of Lahaina, former capital of the Kingdom of Hawaii. I'm fortunate enough to both live and work in Lahaina, where I have access to grocery stores, restaurants, bars, theaters, and a handful of world-class surf breaks all within a short bike ride. I pull into the parking lot at Sacred Hearts School and walk into the faculty lounge to check my mailbox and begin my day.

I find Mary Anna, my older colleague and close friend, sitting at a small table in the center of the room. "We need to talk," she tells me, holding up the front page of the Maui News. Today's headline reads:

MAUI LAND AND PINEAPPLE COMPANY TO BUILD 40 LUXURY HOMES AND A GOLF COURSE ON LIPOA POINT

"There's no way in hell," I tell Mary Anna. "Can they even do that?"

"It's their land," she says. "They can do whatever they want with it."

I take the newspaper out of Mary Anna's hands and read as she looks on. The article says something about needing to respond to the dwindling economy. With the value of the land and the desirability of the location, the article says, the proposed development is a quick and necessary option to quell stockholder anxiety, save ML&P from going under, but most important (they always lie), "it's about creating good paying jobs."

"Nobody will stand for this," I tell Mary Anna before I've even finished reading. I look up at the clock and notice that it's about time to head down to my classroom. I place the newspaper back on the table, writing it off as impossible.

"It finishes by saying," Mary Anna explains, "that the area is poorly managed and that this is important for preserving it."

"With mansions and a golf course? Please." I recall doing maintenance for a golf course during college, and the ridiculous amount of pesticides involved, chemicals that pose grave dangers to fragile underwater ecosystems. "There will be a riot."

"You're damn right there will be a riot. We should have our students protest it."

"What do you mean?"

"I have some ideas," Mary Anna says, with some serious rebelliousness and anger in her voice. "I'm going to make opposing this part of the eighth-grade curriculum. I suggest you do the same."

"Part of my curriculum? How?" Mary Anna, who I often call Pollyanna, is the definitive social justice warrior and educator.

She tells me that this Friday, the county council meeting is allowing the public to go on record about the proposal. "Field trip to City Hall," she says. "If ever there was a meaningful lesson on government."

"You're such a hippie," I tell her. "We have a visitor coming that day, but tell you what I'll do: I'll have my fifth graders write some letters to the council. Maybe you can deliver them for us."

"Have them write poems about the bay. I'll have my eighth graders read the best ones."

"When do you want them?"

"In my box by Wednesday."

The first bell reminds us that classes begin in five minutes. Leading a room full of 10-year-olds at seven-thirty in the morning requires some sort of stimulant, so I grab a clean mug from a small baker's rack wedged in the corner of the lounge and pour a cup of coffee followed by a pile of sugar. I wish Mary Anna a good day and walk out the door under the thatched tin roof of the fifth through eighth grade corridor. Every student is excited that summer is approaching, so they're more restless than usual. Some are throwing balls or running around aimlessly while others quiz each other with flash cards. After I unlock my classroom door and enter, I place my messenger bag under my desk and take out my laptop. Twenty years ago, before each school day began, a nun wearing a habit sat at this same desk and read her Bible. Today, it's me sitting here, beginning a Malama Honolua page to add onto our class website. I like to think it's a change that the locals welcome.

When the second bell rings, I turn on the lights and stand outside of my classroom door, smiling at a pile of 5th graders stumbling towards me, their skinny bodies weighed down by mammoth backpacks. They bump into each other and knock over chairs and desks as they herd into the classroom. Most of the girls take their clean-pressed worksheets out of their folders, neatly place them on the tops of their desks, and check their work for errors. The boys throw their backpacks on the ground, and then empty them onto the floor, scrambling for last night's assignments. Several of them, both girls and boys, place their surfboards on a makeshift rack I've built in the back.

I take a look around and calculate the attendance. "Hey! Listen up. Where's Wiseman?" Rhett Wiseman, the teacher's pet, is such a talented surfer he already has corporate contracts with major surf brands.

Johnny McCrea, Rhett Wiseman's best friend, looks at me and asks, "Did you see the waves today, Mr. Ewan?"

"Yes, Johnny. Why?"

"It's big and barreling. Rhett's probably playing hooker."

"That's hooky, Johnny, not hooker." You have to love their innocence.

I take lunch count, send a text-message, and pound my coffee. "I want everyone to line-up outside the classroom in boy-girl order. We have prayer service. You know the drill." Their awkward line splinters and snakes behind me as we walk down to Maria Lanakila, the oldest Catholic Church on the island. I walk next to the line leader, a soft-spoken Native Hawaiian student named Kamaka, who tells me all about fishing with his father over the weekend. He becomes silent as we pass the outside door of the Sacristy and round the front door and walk into the entrance of the church. Kamaka's pointer finger dips into the holy water and he crosses his body. I turn back to look at the other students, place my pointer finger upwards over my lips, and watch their innocent rambunctiousness transform into order, conformed by the sacred ground, or the threat that talking in church means loss of recess.

A few minutes after prayer service, Rhett walks into the classroom with sandy feet and salty hair. I give him an evil glare.

"What?" he asks. He wears a devious smile. "The waves were sick."

"Stop being a kook," I tell him. "Get here on time."

"Sorry, Mr. Ewan."

At the end of the day, Rhett, who struggles in school, stays for extra help before heading down to Lahina Harbor to paddle out and meet his classmates. He sits in a small desk directly across from me. "Seriously dude," I tell him, "you have to get here on time."

"I will. It won't happen again."

"I surfed before school and I made it here. You can too."

Rhett stares at the notebook on his desk and scratches his head. Today, I'm helping him study for an upcoming science quiz on the ranks of biological classification: kingdom, phylum, class, order, family, genus, and species. I teach him the mnemonic device that I learned to memorize their order, where each word in the sentence corresponds with the letter of the rank: "King Phillip came over for give snaps."

"I've got a better one," Rhett says. "Kooky people come over for good surf."

I laugh and tell him, "That's awesome. Whatever works for you."

"It's true, Mr. Ewan. Too many kooks are moving out here." Rhett might be a haole but he was born on this island, and in his short eleven years, he already notices drastic changes to his home. "My parents told me that people are going to ruin Honolua Bay. Is it true?"

"There is a proposal, a plan," I tell him, "to build some big homes and a golf course up there. It's a bad situation. It could really hurt the waves."

Rhett bites down on the pencil in his mouth, takes it out, and then grips it hard with his small hand. "Who would do that?" he asks.

"Kooky people," I tell him.

At four o'clock, after Rhett shuts the door, I pack up my stuff and start driving back towards the bay. When I pull into the parking lot, the only person there is Potts. He picks up a Red Bull can from off the ground and throws it into the bed of his truck.

"Come back for more?" he asks. I'm sort of taken aback that Potts is again initiating a conversation with me.

"Of course. How is it looking?"

"Winds are onshore now. Sloppy and closing out." This explains why the parking lot is empty.

"Is it true about the development?" I ask him, hoping he'll tell me it's nothing but a proposal, still trying to convince myself that the world doesn't really work this way.

"I've worried this day would come," he says.

"Can't we do something? I mean eighty percent of this island surfs. Nobody will stand for this."

"First, we have to do a better job of managing this place ourselves," Potts tells me. "We can't give them any ammo against us."

Potts explains that he's going to start organizing a coalition, holding meetings, and begin cleaning any rubbish in the area. He tells me about his plans to build a natural staircase out of local materials to stabilize the trail down, believing that ML&P is going to cite its current condition as a potential liability, and one that the development will do a better job of "managing," but with cement and rebar instead of kiave and sandalwood. I tell Potts that I'd like to help, so he writes down his email for me, then shakes my hand. "This is our kuleana. An opportunity for us to take care of the 'aina," he tells me. "If we don't honor it, then they'll keep claiming that they have to do it for us."

Instead of driving back to town, I make a left out of the parking lot and head towards Windmills, a more isolated surf spot about a mile or so on the opposite side of Lipoa Point. I'm hopeful that the winds, now blowing in the opposite direction from this morning, will be offshore at Windmills, making perfect cylindrical barrels for me to play in. When I get there though, I see only one truck parked on the side of the road. Assuming that the waves are junk, I leave my board in the truck as I head down to check out the conditions.

Supposedly, ML&P had some windmills in a large clearing here until 1946, when a tsunami struck Maui and took them all out. Today, the trail down towards the surf break—far safer than the path at the bay—wanders through what looks like an arboretum with Cook pines, coconut palms, and ironwoods swaying in the Kona winds.

Windmills is hands down the most dangerous place I've ever surfed. There are two hollow waves—a left and a right—that peel over an urchin-covered reef before unloading into a conveyer belt channel, which then sucks all the water back out into the open Pacific. Even on a higher tide, the surf zone is a minefield of knifelike coral heads waiting to puncture anything they come into contact with, be it Lycra or flesh. This place is a true testing ground for even the most seasoned surfers.

On a rocky shelf, a few feet from where we exit the ocean at Windmills, there's a surfboard cemetery, a pile of shattered fiberglass and mangled Styrofoam. Broken boards range from hand-shaped 1960 single fins to the latest epoxy molds. Because big wave surfing requires some poise and control in elements that should evoke panic and fear, it's easy to get wrapped up in the thrills out there, though whenever I paddle out at this place, the surfboard cemetery reminds me of who's really in charge.

I look out into the ocean and notice a lone silhouette scratching towards a monstrous set of waves. When they meet, he reels back, reconsiders, and then strong arms into the pitch. He makes his drop too late, flails down the face, and though he attempts to recover at the bottom, his board buckles on impact as he's sent flying into the reef. Clearly shaken, he rides the remains to shore. He carries the board like it's a limp corpse and lays it to rest among the other carcasses. His eulogy is short: a few, well chosen, four letter words.

"Tough break," I tell him.

"This sucks," he replies. "That was a great board." A fair obituary.

I imagine that miles away in a sterile boardroom, developers who don't surf are writing their own obituary for this hallowed burial ground, consisting mainly of mansions, fairways, and lots of zeros next to their dollar signs. I honestly don't have a clue if they can be stopped. These people live to excavate the sanctity from this Earth, and in their brief time here, they usually get their way.

Before I go back to grab my board, I watch yet another massive wave unloading over the reef, with not one soul in the water to claim it. The dwindling opportunities to surf this place alone—the clear water, thriving reef, and hollow waves—become a looming reality. I sprint to my truck and then back down the trail, board in hand.

As I'm paddling out, I look back at the beach and notice a local fisherman coming down to catch his dinner, as so many locals must do to survive. When I think about the valuable jobs needed for the construction and maintenance of forty luxury homes and a golf course, when I think about an island culture struggling to survive in this dwindling economy, the reasons for developing Honolua become as vast and confounding as the wilderness surrounding it. I find some peace in knowing that while this land may disappear beneath a putting green, the waves that shaped this place will never cease—another reminder of who is really in charge out here.

My Father, The Turtle, and the Bomb
kaylie saidin

When I was a little girl, my father showed me the sea turtles that swam outside the break in Hōnaunau Bay. They were broad-shouldered, and their shells looked ancient, moving lazily through the salty water that stung my eyes. They flapped their leathery arms with efficient ease and stared at us from their eyes on the side. I always felt strange when I looked into those eyes, as if they knew something I didn't.

When I asked my father if the turtles knew things, he told me they did. They had lived much longer than me already and had seen things I may never see. They carried things with them as they swam. My father called them *honu*, the Hawaiian word, and for a long time I did not know any other.

"When I was growing up here," my father said to me, "there were no *honu* on the islands. I never saw them."

"How come?"

"They were hunted to make turtle soup."

I let out an involuntary shudder.

My father would let me ride on his back as he swam the breast-stroke out to sea, moving his arms in a flowing rounded arc in front of him. The hot Big Island sun bore down on my small shoulders and his bronzed back.

He was a strong swimmer before he had the neck injury, and back then, I was too small to swim out past the break on my own. Now I am a better swimmer than he ever was.

When we got to where the water lapped calmly and the waves no longer threatened to crash over our heads, he would let me off his back, and we would dive under to see the *honu*. This was where they lived.

My father taught me a rule: never touch the *honu*. We carry germs that their bodies cannot handle. And humans must always leave nature be. Do not be like the tourists who come here and sunbathe and smoke on the sacred land and touch the *honu* and step on the *vana*. Do not be like your mother, whose pale freckled skin burns in the sun, who cannot understand a pidgin accent. You are half of me, and you are going to learn to do things the right way.

Once, I was on Sandy Beach with my parents on a Saturday, watching the older kids body board. I was at the age where I was still young, around ten years old, but not too young to notice those around me doing things that I wasn't old enough to do yet.

A group of locals from the upper school dove in and out of the barreling surf. I had seen them there before. Their skin was a deep, rich brown from the sun, and I longed for mine to look that way too.

I watched one girl, maybe fifteen, catch a wave. She flew down the center of it sideways, her face full of glee, then stood up crouching on the little beater board she rode. Arms out in front of her, as if she was doing a dance, and holding on to the side of the foam, the wave curled around her. I watched intently until I saw her come out on the other side. Her friends congratulated her, and I envied her height, her freedom to be at the beach without her parents, her sheer strength, visible from the muscles on her back and shoulders, swimming through the frothing shore break.

I was sucking on the end of my French braid my mother had twined. It tasted like salt. My mother sat behind me, reading a book and wearing big sunglasses that I always thought made her look like a bug. Her freckled skin was covered in sunblock. I moaned as she forced me to put it on.

"Mom," I said. "I don't want to put it on. It's not that hot out."

My mother was from Boston, with fiery red hair, green eyes, and freckles. She had met my father on a work trip in Honolulu and never left. Unlike many, she had never adopted the perpetual tan that residents achieve. She lathered herself in coconut scented drugstore sunscreen every day, without fail. Then, without my consent, she would lather me. I would stand and allow myself to be covered from head to toe in sunscreen, feeling humiliated at my youth.

I watched the older kids surfing in the shore break on their foam boards as my mother rubbed my back with the white goop.

"Mom," I said again. "I want to surf."

"We can get you a board. Uncle Isaiah has that extra one in his garage."

My father called to me from the water where the tide pools were. "Hey, kiddo!" I didn't hear him at first. He called again: "K!"

My name was Kea, but back then, it was always kiddo or K.

I got up, stumbling a little bit in the hot sand. My legs had been getting longer than I remembered, and I felt like an awkward bird walking around, tripping over my feet. My father was kneeling down by the lava rock, his hands pressed together, cradling something.

"Want to see something?" he asked.

"What is it?"

"Look."

He spread his hands out, and in them was a tiny octopus, barely bigger than his two palms. It squirmed and writhed and was a deep purple.

"It's a *he'e*," he said, which meant octopus.

For some reason, I felt an intense fear inside me as I watched it. Unlike the *honu* that swam a distance from us, it seemed to struggle in my father's leathery hands. I watched the tentacles fold over onto one another, and I wondered where its eyes were.

"Where did you find it?" I asked.

"Over under that rock."

"Was it alone?"

"Yes," he said. "But this is a baby *he'e*. I'm sure it has a family close by."

I closed my eyes and suddenly felt dehydrated. Maybe it was from the saltwater. But then again, maybe not. Panicked, I stared down at the creature that wriggled in the grasp of my father.

"Put it back," I said. Then, without meaning to or knowing how to stop myself, I started to cry. "Put it back under the rock, Dad."

He looked confused. "K, what's wrong?"

I was silent in my childhood inability to articulate what was wrong. I continued to sob, feeling small, much smaller than I felt when my mother forcefully rubbed sunscreen on my back. Finally, I managed to tell him: "It has a family. We took it from them. Put it back. It has to go back."

My father was hesitant, but at the same time, it seemed he understood. He placed the *he'e* in my hands, and it wrapped itself around my forearm. Together, we knelt down, ankle deep in the tide pools. I let the creature go into a small, water-filled crevice where it climbed down from me and disappeared into the lava rock.

A little bit later, we left the beach and went to get shaved ice, and I sat in silence as my parents chattered over the local radio.

I thought about how on the Big Island, there was the old site of a *pu'uhonua*—a place of refuge—that I'd been to. In the days before early settlers had come to the islands, Hawaiians who broke an ancient law could avoid death by fleeing to the place of refuge. There, they could absolve their crimes with the gods. I thought of the huge, carved wooden *tiki* statues of the *ki'i* protector gods that loomed on the edge of the site. I thought I felt them watching me, their open mouths drawn, angry eyes glaring.

We got out of the car in the parking lot and my father held the door open for me.

"I'm sorry, Kea," he said. I knew he meant it because he said my whole name. "You're right. I didn't think about the *he'e* or his family. I just wanted to show you it."

"It's okay."

"You're different than I was at your age," he told me. "I held a lot more anger. You are wiser, and stronger, and kinder."

I couldn't imagine my father as a child my age, so I just imagined the him I knew in the body of a ten-year-old. A ten-year-old that could swim well.

"I'm sure that's not true, Dad."

Many years later, when I was a teen, I would find out that it was true.

I would hear stories of my grandfather, someone who existed only in my hazy memory. He was a tiny Hawaiian man, bony and short but stout, with faded warrior tattoos covering his arms. I would hear that he beat my father's mother while my father watched, that he did not approve of my mother. That when he came to my father's college graduation, he did not know what my father had majored in. And after hearing this, I would replay the incident with the octopus in my head, looking for signs that my father did not know the meaning of the word family but was trying to find it in me.

I left to go to the mainland for college, much to the displeasure of my friends. I broke the news to them that I was leaving Hawai'i while we played video games at Sam Tsiki's house on the North Shore. He was the only one of us that had a playroom in his house. The room had one large couch and a matching love seat, the foam inside showing through scratches created by his two large dogs. The walls were covered in posters, J Boog and a big Eddie Aikau one that read in block letters, *Eddie Would Go*. A Kanaka Maoli flag hung above the television, green and yellow and red with crossed oars in the center, the emblem of the Hawaiian separatist movement. We made fun of him for the flag a lot.

"Brah," we'd say. "Sam. You know you're not native, huh? You're Japanese."

"I'm local. I'm Hawaiian. And we gotta be our own kingdom again."

"Your ancestors came here to farm sugar cane after colonization, stupid ass. This becomes the kingdom of Hawai'i again and you're *pau*."

To which Sam would say, "*ainokea*." Which meant that he didn't care.

When I told them I was leaving at the end of that summer, they were almost angry with me. "You're gonna hate it," they said. "Californians think they're better than everyone. Those kooks don't even know how to surf. And the water will be so cold you have to wear a wetsuit."

I stared at the rug. I had already thought about all of this before. I had sat at the kitchen table with my father all night, the hot air coming through the screen door next to us, the B-52 roaches with the long-hooked antennae swarming outside. We had talked all night about the logistics of moving to the mainland. I knew what I had to do.

"I don't think San Diego is all that different," I said.

They laughed and laughed. "You may be *hapa*," said Sam. "But you're still a *haole* deep down in there."

Haole was an insult. It meant foreigner. It meant *without breath*. I knew it was a joke, but this time it felt personal.

Come September, I fit my entire life into a large suitcase checked out of Honolulu International Airport.

My parents followed my lead soon thereafter, moving up north to the San Francisco Bay. "Hawai'i isn't the same anymore," said my father. "It's too expensive. Too many people. Waikiki is like Disneyland now. Nothing is local anymore."

"Not even us," I said.

He looked at me, side-eyed. "Did your friends tell you that? Don't listen to them. There's a wide world out there that isn't those islands."

I said nothing.

"And you know, San Diego really isn't that different from here anyway."

"I know, Dad."

In college, I got a summer job as an ocean lifeguard. It seemed the obvious choice—I had been swimming and surfing my entire life, and the few other Hawaiian kids I knew in my classes did the job, too. I wanted to fit in with them, wanted them to like me and see me as authentic, even though I was just a *hapa* and I couldn't surf as well as they did.

I ended up stationed in Imperial Beach, the farthest city south just before the marshland and never-ending shoreline became Mexico. The ocean in California was not like Hawai'i, I learned quickly. The water was cold and startling, not as salty, and the floor was sandy and rocky with rarely any reef.

As I learned to duck dive under waves wearing fins and carrying a life preserver, I would scream once I was under them to adjust to the cold. I would surface and begin my freestyle, one arm over the other, keeping my head out of the water. I would imagine someone drowning, probably a child, stuck in the riptide and swept out to sea. I would finally reach the buoy, the imaginary victim, and practice yelling: "Hey, I'm a lifeguard."

The miles of running on the soft sand beach that stretched northward did not phase me, nor did the repetitive swims around the rock jetty. I felt my muscles tighten and my skin bronze and my swim stroke get stronger. In fact, nothing phased me until the very last day of training, when we had to jump from the pier.

Part of the training was to launch yourself off the pier, with no hesitation and with your arms above your head holding your tube and fins. It must have been around fifty feet down, and I was the last in the training group to go. I stared down at the dark water, reflecting the June gloom clouds that loomed ahead. If I were in Hawai'i, it would be clear, and I would see fish swimming and maybe even *honu*. But here, there was nothing but the dark sloshing of the waves rolling through the frigid Pacific.

"Jump," my boss said. He was right behind me.

"I can't."

"You have to."

This continued for a long time until I was almost crying. I suddenly felt the way I did when I was a child, when I got too tired from being in the sun or after my father had showed me the octopus. The training group waited in the water below me, staring up, and I looked down at them, willing my body to move but it was refusing.

Finally, my boss said, "If you don't jump, we can't let you be an ocean lifeguard."

So I jumped, at last. My body hit the cold water with a slap, and I swam to shore, where I ran back on the hardened sand, distant from the group. I had never been so embarrassed.

When I got home, I called my parents. They wanted to know how my training had gone. My mother picked up.

"Hey, Kea," she said. "Congratulations. We're really proud of you."

For some reason, it sounded like my mother was running.

"Thanks," I told her. "But you shouldn't be. We had to jump from the pier, and I took thirty minutes to work myself up to it. I cried in front of my boss."

"Oh, man. I'm sorry, K," she said. She sounded distant, faraway and distracted.

"What's wrong, mom?"

There was a pause. Then she said, "Your father has been in the hospital lately."

I felt my stomach plunge, my heart settle somewhere in my throat. I felt myself jump from the pier and the falling sensation never stopped, sinking farther and farther under the water.

"What happened?" I asked. I imagined him paralyzed after bodyboarding at Sandy's. I imagined him lost at sea, like in the movies. The Coast Guard taking four days to find him.

"He has a slipped disk in his neck," she said. "It started being painful, so we took him to the doctor. He has to get some surgery, or at least some pain reliever."

"Is he okay?" I asked.

"Yeah," she said. "He'll be okay."

We were never a family of many words. We spoke in subtleties, hidden codes and meanings that it seemed we all understood. Or at least I thought we did. My parents traversed their lives under the surface of the water, silent, like submarines. When I got older, I realized it was possible that we all meant and felt completely different things and that, in that respect, I was completely alone.

It's easy to look back on the things that happened and see the poetic coincidences about them, and even easier for a nostalgia-ridden mind to betray the truth. I would like to describe my father injuring himself while he hiked up Diamond Head or sailing in an outrigger canoe through Polynesia. I would like to imagine that I became an ocean lifeguard as a response to his ultimate loss against Mother Nature, that I learned to swim while he sank, that as he grew brittle I grew into the space he once filled. I would like to see the connection in all of this.

But the truth was that my father's neck and upper spine had been hurting him for a long time, and like an animal hiding to lick its wounds, he had remained the silent backbone of the household. By the time the pinched nerve finally became unbearable, he was sitting on the couch, playing Scrabble with my mother.

Scrabble, for God's sake. They may as well have been in a nursing home. I wondered when, in the time that I had been away, my parents had suddenly grown so old.

I took time off from lifeguarding and visited my parents that summer. Despite his attempts to hide it from us, my father's sickness was slow and eating at him. He slept on the couch with a bag of ice resting against his neck. The left side of his mouth would not turn upwards when he smiled. We drove to the cold and windy Northern California beach; I put on my wetsuit and paddled out into the fog and seaweed. He watched from the beach, unable to swim, unable to follow.

"Kea," he told me. "Don't ever grow old."

"I can't help it," I said.

He looked like an old turtle, receding into his shell. Watching me from the side, with prey-situated, drowning, all-knowing eyes.

Ten years after college, long after I had returned to Oahu, I was on Interstate 72 going through Waimanlo, stuck in traffic for the morning commute. The January sun had risen, the myna birds were raucous in the banyan trees, and as I passed by the beach, I saw that the winter surf was pumping. I fought every urge in my body to call in sick–I had already done so a week before for the same reason—or to call my favorite coworker and beg him to take my shift. I would have given anything to spin my truck around, drive back home, and wax my board.

I sat, humming along to the local radio that hadn't changed. Some things had, some things hadn't. I was surprised at the fact that for the most part local stayed local.

I was startled to hear a buzzing noise on my phone that I had never heard it make before. Looking down, I saw the white screen and all-capital text I had seen only in flash-flood warnings before:

BALLISTIC MISSLE THREAT INBOUND TO HAWAII. SEEK IMMEDIATE SHELTER. THIS IS NOT A DRILL.

I read it over twice, three times. Then I looked around me and saw that traffic had come to a complete stop. The reggae music on the radio station was interrupted by a message that sounded pre-recorded.

The robotic, eerily calm voice instructed listeners. "If you are outdoors, seek immediate shelter in a building. Remain indoors well away from windows. If you are driving, pull safely to the side of the road and seek shelter in a nearby building or lie on the floor. We will announce when the threat has ended."

I put my truck in park, grabbed my keys and bag, and got out of the car. Up and down the highway, other people were exiting their vehicles too. I heard the terrified, hyperventilating voices of those who had moments before been stuck in traffic with me.

"Oh my God," a large woman in front of me was saying to no one in particular. "We're going to get bombed."

"It's not a bomb," said an older white man outside the car beside her, catty-corner to mine. "It's a missile. It's headed for us. I knew this day would come. The fucking North Koreans."

Around me, people were sitting down, shielding themselves under their car. Children's voices were asking: "Mom, what's going on?" "Hush *keiki*, it's okay." Someone had begun praying loudly. Around the white noise of voices, I almost felt silence.

I stepped over the guardrail of the highway and into the brush. Abandoning my vehicle, I made my way down to the beach. There was no one there, nothing but the sound of the wind on the ocean and the screeching birds that had no idea the world was ending.

I opened my phone and called my dad. He picked up on the first ring.

"Hey, Kea," he said. He sounded tired. "What's up?"

At my feet, below the leather flip flops, I noticed something wriggling in the white coral sand. Kneeling down, resting my phone in the crevice between my ear and collarbone, I realized there were tiny eggs beneath me.

"Nothing," I said to my father. "I was just thinking about you. I wanted to see how you were."

I could tell he was smiling, or at least, with the one half of his face that was able to. He had been in a wheelchair, paralyzed for years now.

"I'm okay," he said. "Same old."

"Me, too," I said. Beneath my feet, tiny *honu* were hatching and climbing from the membrane of their eggshells. Writhing in the sand, they began their instinctive journey down to the water.

"You'll never guess what I'm doing right now," I said.

"What?" There was that excitement in his voice, the longing for a time he no longer had in a place he was no longer a part of.

"I'm watching *honu* hatch."

"Really?"

"Yeah."

"They must be leatherbacks," he said. "It's too early for the usual *honu*. That's a big deal. You almost never see leatherbacks."

I watched the tiny *honu* crawl down the shoreline and I followed alongside them. They were determined to reach their home.

My father continued talking. "Make sure you protect them from the birds," he was saying. "The birds try to eat baby *honu* after they hatch on the beach."

Seagulls and myna were flocking, it was true, but they did not come near me. I hovered above the group of *honu* children, blocking them from the sunshine and the predators. At last, they reached the place where the slow waves met the golden sand and crossed over into the sea.

"Thanks," I said. "I think they're home now."

"They'll grow up. Maybe sometime you'll see them out there when you surf."

"Yeah. Maybe." I paused. The world was ending, the bomb was coming, and I felt as though a strange gaze, a magnified eye, was watching me. "I gotta go to work, Dad."

"Me, too." He laughed. This was a joke—he hadn't worked in years.

"Take care of yourself," I told him. Then I hung up.

I walked back to the highway slowly and was surprised to see traffic had begun moving again. Looking down at my phone, I saw a second emergency alert: THERE IS NO MISSLE THREAT OR DANGER TO THE STATE OF HAWAII. REPEAT. FALSE ALARM.

One of the times when I rode out to sea cross-legged on the back of my father to see the *honu*, we saw something different.

I followed him out into the clear water, swimming alongside him with just my goggles on. I could free dive pretty deep—I was a little bit older by then—and was showing my father how far I could go when we spotted one.

This *honu* was smaller than most I'd seen, and I noticed that it was swimming strangely and had difficulty moving off the ocean floor. My father dove down to it, about six and a half feet, then returned to me. He motioned for me to surface.

"It's got a rope around it's fin," he said. "It must have gotten caught in a trap."

My father reached into the pocket of his swim trunks and took out his dive knife. He told me when I was older, I should never swim or dive without one. Then he handed it to me and said, "We have to go cut it off."

I had never held a knife before, and I made sure to hold it arm-distance away from me. I swam down to the ocean floor with my father and approached the *honu*. I thought that I would look into its eyes and see animalistic fear, but I saw nothing but the wise, familiar gaze. I wondered if this had happened before to the turtle. I wondered if this *honu* simply knew that situations like this happened sometimes, without ever being in one. I wondered if it knew that everything that was to happen had already happened and that something was happening right now and that moment of something was nothing and everything at once. I wondered what it knew that I didn't.

My father held my arm and put his giant hand over mine, encompassing it. He guided me to the rope and began to pick at it carefully. The twine broke surprisingly easily; it had loosened in the warm water. I watched as my father pulled the rope off the *honu*, and then it swam away from us. The bubbles in my chest were forcing me up and I rose to the surface. When I went back under, the *honu* was gone. My father remained, and I handed him the knife.

We swam back to shore, and I did not ride on his back. I was next to him, taking long strokes and kicks with my legs extended and my arms below the water as he did.

Looking for Power

chad w. lutz

The Foothills

I've been looking for a power source, somewhere to charge. I don't know how else to let people know I'm alive. I spent most of the morning scaling the rubble downtown, but all I could find was an old payphone with no dial tone. I was so upset I tried to eat my iPad. Now I'm hungry and my gums hurt. It's terrible. An actual tragedy. I haven't checked my Tweets since Tuesday. It's killing me.

And that's what's getting to me: the gravity of the situation. I can't do anything without thinking it's special or important, even though I know that isn't true.

Everything is gone. Steel poles jut out of the ground like crooked fingers bent in every direction. Small fires burn, unbridled, in places they shouldn't, like the tops of streetlights and along telephone wires; the middle of Lake Merritt is on fire; on Telegraph, I saw a wounded cat burn its whiskers trying to lick its tail out.

The only thing that's helped me through the last eight hours is imagining everything I see in my favorite Instagram filters.

It makes everything seem a little less like it is.

Sacramento

Someone from Sacramento says what I saw travels in packs.

"You don't know shit," I tell them.

Shit fills their eyes and they fire back with, "That's exactly what people who don't make it say," and then really start laughing.

I'm hugging my iPad as close to my body as I possibly can. Clothes dusted and caked with gore, and ask, "You mean people who don't find outlets?" because now that everything's destroyed, this guy might be all that matters.

"Look around," they say, gesturing at the remains of the Tribune building and a pile of Uber cars, "Where do you think you're going to find an outlet?"

"Huh?"

"I said, 'Where do you suppose we'll find one?'"

To be honest, I don't know a thing about this guy. Maybe humanity bands together for salvation or something in the end, whatever; but, judging by the thick black cloud in the sky, a mixture of concrete, people, and fire, I know we're further down the food chain, and that this guy could easily just be the most desperate person he's encountered. For all I know he strings his mother out every night with his fists.

"I never thought of it like that before," I say, messing with a street sign discarded like a playing card. It's Lakeshore. Sacramento makes shoeprints in the dust.

"Who do you think cleans this up?" he says, tired or bored or something, but I ignore him. He knows damn well no one just cleans something up like this. The Romans know it, the Greeks know it. Seattle knows it. Chicago. New York. London. Paris.

After a minute in silence, he asks, "Do you think Snap-Chat still exists if no one uses it?" and my eyes light up instantly.

"You have battery?" I ask, practically leaping out of my pants.

He pulls out his phone and says, "No, I was just wondering," but I can clearly see the screen light up as he slips it into his pocket.

I grip my iPad. I trace its edges. I say, "It's comforting to think the Internet is still out there," and scoot closer.

"Why?" he asks.

I'm so excited I yelp. "It means I'm not alone," I say, picking nervously at my thigh, "It's been so long, you know?"

Sacramento stares at me, flatly, like he's waiting for a punch. When whatever it is he's waiting for doesn't come he says, "Really? It's been six hours."

"Six hours; six days," I say, "What's it to you, anyway?" I'm smiling so hard it hurts.

Sacramento holds up his wristwatch, saying "A lot," and points. "About a hundred and thirty-eight hours. Maybe the world."

So, I leave.

I can't take this kind of abuse. Not during the apocalypse. I'll give him the fact we're both upset over the world ending, sure; but if Sacramento thinks I'm going to just idle through the rest of eternity listening to bullshit insane negativity, he's got another thing coming.

I don't look back. I keep walking. Walking with my iPad. Looking for an outlet. Looking for some power. I think about what my mother, who told me "Never trust anything anyone from Sacramento says," and here I am getting worked. Not anymore.

A year goes by. A week. Who's to say? Four hours? I don't own a wristwatch, my phone is somewhere at the bottom of the Bay, and the digital thermometer on the Wells Fargo building downtown doesn't exist anymore.

A whatever later, I catch up with Sacramento in Fruitvale. I've changed my mind, but it's too late. Their head is missing. Or something. I don't know. They're very dead, and when I can't find a pulse, I steal his phone. Not like he'll be needing it. In fact, he kind of owes me.

I post a picture of the body on Facebook with the caption: #aliveinoakland and instantly regret the irony, but the moment it posts, it hits me: it's still out there, and by it, I mean everything, the world. Paris. London. New York. It's all still there, and it's wonderful.

I fly through my newsfeed. I scroll and scroll and scroll and scroll. I don't think I've ever had this much fun looking in on other peoples' lives in my entire life. Everything looks normal outside the Bay. News aggregates are reporting a contained event. Surrounded by suffering, I've never felt so much relief. I've never been so happy to be me.

I'm just about to send a message to my mom when the battery light flashes and the phone dies. I hit the side of it with my hand, and, of course, nothing happens, so, I shake it and the lights flicker but I can't get them to come back on. Damnit. Now the only proof I'm alive is a photo of a dead Sacramentan.

Progeny

Just before nightfall, a young man approaches me with a child at his side, a daughter. He looks me dead in the eye and asks if rocks are edible. When I tell him no, he lets out this huge sigh, plops down cross-legged, and apologizes to his kid, a child of no more than four. When the kid asks why, the man just shakes his head, buries his face in his hands, and sobs until spit trickles through his fingers.

I don't know what it is. Maybe it's the absence of orange light pollution, or the brilliance of the stars overhead, but I don't feel good about myself watching this father cry into his hands like that. I feel like all the world is draining out of that man's eyes, and the only way to dry the world's bleeding is to dry this man's tears.

So, I grab him gently by the shoulder and I say, "They travel in packs," like I know what I'm talking about. I tell him I've never seen so many. "Tens of thousands of them," I say, "like a waterfall in the sky shooting this way and that."

His voice trebles in the new darkness. I can't tell what he's saying, but I don't care. I'm just glad there's something. Not just for me, but for the sake of his daughter.

I leave.

Seminary

I've never been to Mills College before, but I follow them on Instagram, and the campus always looked gorgeous. Now, I'm on a hill toward the back of the seminary. There's an old ceremonial chimney that somehow survived everything, and I've made a small fort in its hearth. Looking around at the tall, wispy grasses and downed oak trees, I imagine it in Mayfair. Mayfair is one of my favorite filters.

It's getting cold. I'm cold. I've been cold. I've been cold for days. I'm still shaking off what Sacramento said about time, the jerk. What a way to meet someone.

Through my tears, I see the sunset, golden-orange on the horizon. I think tomorrow may not be better, but it will at least be day.

I can see the entire Bay from up here, and it's true, the entire region is in ruins. San Jose, Palo Alto. Gone. The Golden Gate Bridge. Sales Force. Coit Tower. Sutro. All of it, crumbled asphalt and debris, the only evidence anyone was ever here.

I gasp, imagining the cry of eight million people at once. I laugh until I can't breathe. I fall asleep staring at my iPad, the reflection of the stars.

poem

After 30 Years I Still Like the Idea of Lighting Up

david js pickering

My husband says he'll have his next one
the day he turns 80, the same way he says
he'll ram the final idiot car in front of him

the day he surrenders his keys. Old enough
now for what-the-fuck fantasies of older men,
we're finding our way into later-middle age,

style intact, eyes on the 401(k), Medicare
our highest aspiration. We see Emerald City
floating ahead in a happy blue haze, opium

pipe dream in a poppy-red field Van Gogh
would have painted if he had art directed
at MGM. He would have loved burning

Atlanta the same year, would have doled
speed to Judy Garland, *Here, kid, this'll keep
those heels clickin'*, as Scarlett and Rhett

drove home through murky backlot plumes
to a disheveled Tara, *God as mah witness,
I'll nevah...*   go back to my office again,

negotiate the parking lot's fuming-cherry
gauntlet, the Designated Smoking Place,
catch a whiff and wonder if I'd still smoke

menthols (frenched, of course), lazy wisps
drifting mouth-to-nose and exhaled in rings
of Dietrich ennui, spinning ghost-threads

around faces that twist my resting body
just before sleep, the stuff no positive self-
talk, spiritual work, amends ever quite gets,

such insistent pentimento. Why not wrap it
again in silver-blue brume, watch it float on
the exhale? I'm way beyond legal now

with a wallet full of cash – just what I used
to cruise as a kid, my pack sitting on the bar,
needy-eyed and looking for a light. How odd

to lock eyes with him, to know what awaits
that boy and to wish him well. I don't know
about you, but there's a lot I would change.

nonfiction

Gethsemane for Beginners

charlotte van werven

Loving a foster kid is like loving someone with a terminal illness. The difference is, when a foster kid leaves you, you have no idea whether or not they'll be smiling with family every Christmas, or if they'll end up selling cigarettes on a street corner. You don't know if you'll read their name on a police report or, maybe worse, pass them in the park on some sunny day and not recognize them.

In September of my senior year of high school, my family received news that we'd get our first foster placement. Miracle was supposed to be a short-term case. *Three months*, his social worker said between clicks of her acrylic nails on our wooden tabletop. We would be his second foster family, our home his fourth.

Miracle was a grungy two-and-a-half-year-old boy with blonde hair to his waist and enough swagger to contest any toddler. I expected foster kids to be hesitant and shy. *He might not look you in the eye*, we were warned.

But when Miracle walked through our door, patchy red and marshmallow cheeked, his chin was up, his tangled hair lying down his back, his sticky hands clenched in fists by his jean shorts, three sizes too big. He wore Velcro tennis shoes with holes along the seams. My parents bought him brand new shoes at Fred Meyer on their way home. My dad sized up shoes next to his feet while my mom distracted him with Cheerios.

"Do you want to wear your new shoes, Miracle?" my mom asked with an overly-assuring smile.

He shook his head and popped a few more Cheerios into his mouth, lips stained with Kool-Aid and sprinkled in potato-chip salt.

She took a heavy breath and set the new shoes on the ground. He traipsed into the kitchen, where my two sisters, brother, and I were waiting with stiff backs. The dull rubber throb of his shoes covered the sounds of the whirring dishwasher and the cat licking his paws.

"Hi, Miracle," I finally ground out with a small wave and the most genuine smile I could come up with. His silver dollar eyes met mine and watched me for a minute. I felt scratchy.

"Okay," I said abruptly. "I'm Charlotte." I waved at him again and left the room on limp legs as he glared at the rest of my family.

He seemed comfortable, yet he was coiled tight, something like the silence before someone gives you bad news. But everything was fine for the first few hours as he putted around the house. He ran his hands lightly over an embroidered pillow on the couch, scuffed his feet on our clean carpet, squinted at the posed family photos framed around the walls. He was calm until my mom tried to give him a bath.

I've never heard another kid scream like that.

But once he was clean and dressed in blue footy pajamas, he reestablished his space with arms spread wide. He spun around the living room, one hand clutching the hand of a stuffed toy my brother gave him, his hair, wet and matted, bouncing around his shoulders. Much later, we would find out that his parents believed his hair was magical, like Rapunzel's, and they were afraid he would lose his magic if they cut it off.

As he twirled around the living room, we were all entranced. We gathered around him like he was a campfire—hands held out tentatively toward the heat.

We waited until morning to brush out his hair. We anticipated the screaming this time.

But we didn't anticipate the nightmares.

When terrors woke him at three a.m. every night, he would whimper *almost* silently in his crib. He started screaming hoarsely when my mom reached out to pick him up. She pulled back her hands, chest heaving, biting her lips closed. He hid his face in his pillow and resumed whimpering. My mom shuddered and walked away.

As much as he wanted to, he couldn't make the nightmares go away by himself. A few weeks in, he started banging his head on the crib when he'd wake up from a dream. He'd hit his head, the crib would hit the wall, and no one would be able to sleep. My dad wrapped blankets around the bars to keep him from hurting himself, but that only made him throw his head back harder.

I, a fierce insomniac, always awake when the banging started, wanted so badly to get up and try to comfort him, but I had to leave it to my parents. That was my job. I was only a kid and he was my brother. But it was hard to breathe when he got like that.

The whole family had tight lungs for a while as we waited for him to adjust. The first morning, my mom sat him down at the kitchen table and set out seven different cereal boxes.

"Do you want Rice Krispies?" she asked, eyes bright.

He blew his lips full of air and stared at his choices.

"Fruit Loops, maybe?" she tried again.

"Corn Chex? Captain Crunch?" She bit her lip and sighed. "How about oatmeal?" she suggested. "Maybe a banana?" He looked up at her and scrunched his eyes. He didn't say a word. She poured a light layer of Rice Krispies in a bowl and added a splash of milk. She passed it to him with a spoon, but he reached in with his fingers, sprinkling milk onto his shirt.

The next day at breakfast my mom tried again, and he pointed to each cereal in turn. She shrugged and poured a small helping of each into the same bowl, swallowing a grimace. He ate.

He ate anything we put in front of him. He even ate raisins and lima beans, much to my dad's amusement. At one dinner my fourteen-year-old sister pushed her peas into a pile and asked if she could have a pass on eating them. My dad grinned and pointed at Miracle's plate.

"If he eats it, so do you," he said cheekily. She rolled her eyes as the toddler shoved peas into his mouth with chubby fingers.

The first food we found he hated was cantaloupe. I had sliced some for my Saturday lunch, and he watched me eat it with watery eyes.

"What're you eating?" he asked, mouth full of celery.

"This? It's called cantaloupe. Do you want some?" I picked up a chunk and dropped it on his plate. He shoved it in as soon as he swallowed the celery.

He started gagging almost instantly, but kept chewing, his little throat bobbing like a frog.

"Miracle!" my mom called out. "Here, spit it out!" She held a napkin under his chin.

He shook his head with fervor and kept chewing. He finished the bite with tears loitering in his eyes.

"Want some more?" my dad joked.

Miracle nodded solemnly and reached out to take some from my plate. My dad opened his mouth to say something but nothing came out. His shoulders slumped as he looked in agony at my mom. She shook her head and closed her eyes.

"You don't have to eat it if you don't like it," my dad told him, nodding emphatically.

"I *do* like it," he insisted.

"I don't think you do," my dad said, pushing his own food around his plate.

"I *do*," Miracle cried out. Tears were now starting to fall.

The rest of us exchanged glances around the table.

He had a full-blown meltdown after that. He cried loudly in his chair for ten minutes before stopping because he'd forgotten what was so upsetting. My mom cleaned him up, and he went to sit on the couch to look at books. The Berenstain Bears were his favorite.

Miracle could sit on the couch for hours flipping through those stories. His eyes glittered as he traced shapes with the tip of his finger. But he never lost sight of the world outside the pages. If someone sat down next to him, he'd jump and move away.

Unlike my siblings, I started on the opposite side of the couch, gradually moving closer every day. After a month or so, I was able to sit right next to him without him flinching. He'd silently hand me a book, and I'd start reading aloud.

It was Kenneth who made me realize how close we'd become. Miracle had already been with us for seven months. Kenneth came in March. He was a year younger than Miracle, and almost completely opposite.

Kenneth needed to be constantly cuddled and held. He would cry if someone put him down or wasn't paying enough attention to him. He couldn't say many words yet, but he called everyone "Mom."

On Kenneth's second day in our home, I was sitting on the floor across from him, rolling a rubber ball back and forth. When Miracle got back from daycare, he saw me rolling the ball with Kenneth and ran over to us. His forehead scrunched up, his chin wobbled, and his eyes got deep and damp. He inched forward on flat feet and folded himself into my lap, blocking my hands from catching the ball. I looked at my mom, wide-eyed.

That was the first time he willingly sat on someone's lap.

A little part inside me felt honored by his jealousy. And that made me feel warm and guilty. It shouldn't have been me. It should have been my mom or dad, or *his* mom or dad. I excused that thought though. Miracle needed me. That's what I told myself.

After living with us a few weeks, Kenneth needed a haircut. That was when Miracle started asking the questions we'd been waiting for.

"Why is my hair long?"

"Because your mom and dad asked us not to cut it," I told him.

After pondering that answer he asked, "Where are your mom and dad?"

"Wayne and Janet are my mom and dad," I told him gently.

"But who's tummy did you come out of?" His little eyebrows met in a mountain.

"Janet's," I said.

I could tell the math didn't make sense to him, but he let it be.

I especially hated it when people made comments about his hair.

My great grandma would shake her head of curlers and say, "It's just too bad he looks like a little girl."

I would bite out, "Grandma, the length of hair has nothing to do with gender."

She would "tsk" and change the subject, only to bring it up again at the next family gathering.

Thankfully, Miracle didn't seem to hear.

"Why do I have long hair?" he asked again one night as I brushed it out before bed.

"Because your mom and dad like it better long," I repeated the given answer.

"How come Kenneth doesn't have long hair?"

"Because his mom and dad like it better short."

I wound his hair into a bun on top of his head, and wrapped it with a ponytail. He winced as it pulled tight.

"Your mom and dad like you to have long hair?" he asked me slowly.

I blew a breath between my lips and considered the answers. "I like it better long," I told him.

He nodded and kept his lips pressed.

"Would you like to cut your hair?" I asked him.

He sat for a minute and then turned to face me. "Maybe someday."

"You're handsome either way," I reminded him.

Positive affirmation was an easy thing to give a kid who asked for nothing.

The summer of 2014 I was packing for college when I found my parents at the kitchen table bent over a folder of paperwork, full bowls of ice cream melting beside them.

"What's that?" I asked.

My dad lifted his eyebrows briefly and looked at my mom. She nodded. "Just some information about Miracle."

"Bad stuff?" I wondered as I pulled out a chair.

My mom snorted and pushed the papers toward me.

"Can I look at this?" I asked.

"I think so. Just don't share it with anyone."

Words like *trauma* and *abuse* and *bipolar disorder* jumped out at me. I cracked my neck as a ball of dread, dense and acidic, turned inside me.

"He's going to be alright, right?"

"We're doing our best," my dad reminded me.

It was only a few days after that that I watched Miracle and Kenneth playing with cars on the living room carpet. They were giggling and making engine-revving sounds. Miracle pointed his car to the car in Kenneth's hand.

"How about they're brothers?" he asked.

"Okay." Kenneth wiggled his shoulders up and down.

"Just like you're my brother," Miracle said before zooming off with his car.

That night, I was standing in the kitchen when Miracle came up to me and asked, "Can I have a hug?"

I wasn't sure I heard him right.

"You want a hug?"

He nodded.

I bent down and opened my arms. He walked into them with confidence. But hugging him was something akin to hugging a sack of flour. His arms were not tight, his head was rammed into my shoulder, and he was going limp. I picked him up and hugged him tighter still. Neither of us were very good at it, and when I put him down, I was shaking.

"I love you," I said.

"I love you, too." He smiled softly at me.

Miracle loved in a way I didn't understand for a long time. He loved people when they earned it. But once he loved someone, he would never stop, and his forgiveness was a constant given.

One night at dinner, Miracle was asking my dad a hundred questions about God and preschool and the house he used to live in. My dad, tired and grouchy from a bad day at work, suddenly snapped, " Stop asking questions! Just eat your dinner, Miracle."

My mom glared at him across the table and he waited a minute before quietly saying, "I shouldn't have lost my temper."

Miracle tilted his head, clay eyes peering through his lashes, and nodded at my dad. "I forgive you," he said.

While I was humbled by his ability to forgive, sometimes I resented it.

His birth parents continued to fail their requirements to get him back, so he was still with us the summer of 2015, two years after he came to us. That was the summer we adopted Kenneth.

The judge was talking to all of us during the adoption and asked Miracle, "Are you next?"

His chin bit back swiftly, eyes bright. "No! I'm going to live with my mom and dad really soon."

"Oh," she said, pressing her lips in silent apology.

For the next few weeks, Miracle made his bedtime prayers all about his mom and dad.

"God, I love my mommy and daddy," he'd say with eyes pinched shut. I don't know if he was reminding God or himself.

I suppose I can't begrudge him for loving the people who gave him life, but some nights when I couldn't sleep I'd imagine running away with Miracle so he wouldn't have to go home. I woke up several mornings to a pillow drizzled with tears I hadn't remembered crying.

That year, the year of Kenneth's adoption, was a big one. I went back to college for my sophomore year, and I was stuck in the fear that the last goodbye I gave Miracle would be the forever one. The social worker kept saying that "any day now" his parents would submit their final paperwork and he would be on track to going home. I called my parents often, and the first thing out of my mouth was, "Any news on Miracle?"

They didn't have much to tell about his parents, but they'd give me updates on how he was changing. That year, he started reading a little, understanding numbers, and making friends. He even started tattling on Kenneth. I grinned all day at that news.

That Christmas break was the hardest break I'd ever had. Every morning I opened my eyes already feeling guilty for wasted time. Going back to school was even worse, because I was going to be studying abroad, and there would be no chance for me to take a weekend trip home to say a last goodbye.

In March, when I was at a hostel in Ireland, my mom told me that Miracle's mom had disappeared. I shouldn't have smiled.

"That's it, right? That's her last chance, right? She doesn't get him ever?"

"I don't know," my mom sighed.

It was glory he was still there when I came home. I gave him the first hug, whispering how much I missed him, how tall he'd grown, and how excited I was to spend the summer with him. I gave my dad the next hug. "I feel so loved," he teased. "Second-best."

I gritted my teeth. "It's different. You know that."

His lip quirked up. "Yeah, I know."

In late June we heard that the attorney for Miracle's dad had recommended he give up his case. What followed was six weeks of chaos. I didn't believe what was happening until we stood in the same courthouse, hearing the same oaths, smiling with the same judge from one year earlier. Miracle was wearing a brand new outfit from Gap. He ran his palms over the crisp button-down and looked up at me. He smiled a smile I have never seen on any other kid.

In November of that year I got a letter from my mom. It was a drawing Miracle had done at school. He had colored all of us with lime grass beneath our feet and an oval sunshine above our heads.

The back was signed, *Love, Miracle.*

poem

After J
katherine van eddy

Look at the way it's rooted so firmly on the page
two lightning strikes extending to sea and sky
even the small one like a downed kite, or the stroller
my daughter has just outgrown. Sometimes in a hurry
to reach *ennemenno p* she skips right over it, or else her tongue
tilts toward her teeth, recalling the 20th letter instead, but it doesn't care,
content to stand bold as a King or subtle as a knife,
unspeakable by two-year-olds. She doesn't know how much
a thousand is, a single law of thermodynamics or how to say kiss
and she doesn't care either, no need to know yet
what comes before her, or after.

Diorama

My kid had to make a diorama for school. I told him the educational system was making a puppet out of him. It was one of the colder slaps for the puppet master to strike, dioramas. They wanted to subject you to the ridiculous, the absurd, give you a *soupcon* of what to expect as an "adult." He didn't understand why I had to say crap like that all the time, which could give the bachelor a pretty clear indication of the thankless work of parenting.

"Are you going to help or not?"

"I guess."

I knew I had to. Usually I tried to sabotage my son's work. But that got me quite the chastisement at the last parent-teacher conferences, so I'd been playing it cool.

"What are we doing?"

"Don't worry about what we're doing. Concentrate on cutting out cardboard strips."

His secretiveness derived, I believe, from the suspicion that I would commandeer the vision once I had it in sight. I asked how the diorama game had changed since my time and he said considerably. Apparently, the arms race of everyday life did not exclude the diorama with kids now breaking out the cosmorama, myriorama, and cyclorama. It had become quite the accidental Renaissance for what was once considered a crude form of nineteenth-century entrainment.

I'd been trying to trick Hedge into committing crimes he was probably guilty of and asked on this occasion if he wanted to sniff some glue. He awkwardly declined. So I stuck the nozzle up my nuzzle, inhaled, and made camera shutters of my eyelids. I asked again, "Don't worry, I'm not your parent's dad—"

"I'm not falling for it, and the more you do weird stuff like this the more it seems like an excuse to get high. Just smoke weed like a normal person. It's okay if you want to get high—"

"No. It's not okay. Don't let anyone tell you it is. Let me just do the other nostril. WHOOO, you sure? That's cool. Just … never mine, er, just call your friends. Say dad's got the glue blues and doesn't want to stick alone. Sing, 'I'm walking on *horse feet*, WOW! And don't it feel *glue!*'"

I passed out, and it was a good thing too, for, I had a prophetic dream that would forever alter the history of dioramas …

I awoke in a snowy field and passed through a thick forest until I arrived at a theatrical town. I was to perform in a play for the Empress' visit. The half-made town was made of plywood with painted facades and peopled by imported peasants. I asked what show I was to perform, and the manager said, "The play you were born to play." The people seemed very pleasant, but each time I'd enter one of the buildings, past the entry, the unfinished walls revealed the snowy woods beyond. The people would become lifeless. I yelled, "It's all right. Come spring, we'll patch that up!" But they'd feign a headache or say nothing at all. At night, from treetops, I watched the towns-folk drift around the woods like spirits. I looked up and saw the Empresses procession course down the horizon like a golden river. The whole town was in attendance. The Empress took her seat and the lights dimmed and I was pushed onstage. "In a little village, near the River Minsk-" but a great laugh-ter erupted. Someone threw a bear cub at me that lunked away followed by the imperial caravan and everyone else. The stage manager shook my hand and assured me the baby bear hitting me was very comical.

"What's the gig today? I picked up some whip cream in a can. You a Whip-It man? Are you sure? Me neither. Now let's, uhhh, have a bowl of whip cream I guess."

He set me out cutting balsa wood tiles while he blowtorched sheets of Styrofoam, undulating hills until he'd melted down a nice hinterland. I told him that I'd had a much similar dream where I'd been an actor in a Potem-kin village. He looked at me blankly, "Oh, that's what we're building and that's why I dreamt it. See, I'm attentive … subconsciously."

I had mad respect for Hedge's choice and made a point not to awesomify it with my esthete insights. It'll make for a weak-ass diorama, but I could tell he appreciated it.

"How did you come by the idea?" I asked.

"It came to me in a dream."

"Shut up."

Part Two

The diorama exhibit proved to be just as decadent as Hedge said it'd be. All we were missing was the Sun King, oh wait, there he is, Versailles in sugar. You had a Santa Maria del Fiore in building blocks, a terracotta Angkor Wat, a vibrating football game of the Battle of Hastings. The novelty of our me-ta-diorama thinned before our eyes into glass. And I, as predicted, received many scurrilous looks from other parents. "Your work sucks and now every-body else's dad thinks I can't handle my beer."

"Well, you shouldn't have shown up drunk."

"I shouldn't have shown up with a sucky diorama and if you think I'm the only parent here that's buzzed, you're more of a naïve fifth grader than I took you for."

A dirt-bike kid with a bowl cut named Trevor sauntered up. "Potemkin," he said, "that's clever, way to find a way out of building a proper diorama. Asshole, you help your son half-ass this piece of shit?"

"Trevor," the wool-vested teacher said, "they get the point." The teacher looked at us and sighed. "What's the explanation for this, Hedge? Is Trevor right? You wanted to half-build everything?"

"Teach," I said, "unlike all these other cigar Lamborghinis you see before you, Hedge practically did all of the work. All I did was cut cardboard strips and balsa wood tiles."

"That's probably why it's half-complete." Teach zinged to Trevor.

"Good one, Teach," Trevor said.

"Shut it, Trevor!" I said. "Give me your address, Teach, and get a second. We're dueling. Take Trevor."

Back home, I popped a few panes out of anger and shame—I also told the window repair guy I'd throw him some business. It was certainly a poor mark on our family.

"Shall we burn it?" I asked.

"No," Hedge said. "Let's keep working on it. One day we'll be able to sell it for some serious moo-la."

"Who to?"

"Model train company looking to expand?"

Final Part

We installed the Potemkin village in the backyard and its imperialism knew no bounds. The neighborhoods, factories, and shops sprouted up in neat rows like a garden of industry. On payday, I'd buy some fancy bugs and Hedge and I would watch them duke it out in the town square. It was like having a Japanese monster movie in your backyard.

"Look what I picked up—morning glory seeds. You ever?"

(Mimes eating them and getting high)

"Yeah, all the time."

"What? You're grounded my man, for life. And that's a *crude* high."

"I'm kidding, but I did pick you up some weed and a pipe."

"Wow, that must have been difficult for a fifth grader."

"I have an age."

"We all do. Now, I want you to jump through the smoke rings I blow." Hedge's hopping inspired me. "I have an idea."

I prowled around anger management group meetings and passed out a card that read,

Want to destroy a city?
Get your Godzilla on in Dioramaville

Only a few pecked at first, but once interest was established, I raised it amongst them until I was able to cull a fat check from an academic that knew everything there was to know about earwigs. It was a tough break for Hedge. He'd grown rather fond of the place.

"How much did she net?"

"I'll tell you when you're eighteen."

After the earwig specialist destroyed all our hard work, it looked as though the egg of enlightenment were cracked upon his head. "I'd tell you to give me a call when the next one's built," he said in an om-like drone, "but I don't think I'll ever feel anger again. You got something special here, and if you intend to make a business of it, I'd like a buy into that dream factory."

It all looked good for a second. Building model villages and selling them to eccentric academics to destroy. But then Teach and Trevor showed up for the duel that we had a hell of a time scheduling. "What kind man brings a fifth grader to a duel? Let's go, buddy. TEACH, Teach, I'm going to shoot you in the shoulder for what you wrote in the margins in Hedge's essay on geckos!"

"The only gecko here is you."

"That tears it!"

We charged our laser guns and walked to the center of the decimated Russian village. Twelve steps, turn!

But Teach was a bad shot. Teach heatbeamed me right in the third eye, and his gun wasn't on the duel setting. While the cop drones pursued a fleeing Teach, Trevor cradled me in his arms, and I said to Hedge, "Mmm, manslaughter money, that'll hold you up for a bit. If you run out you can go to Mike Stock. He'll put you up doing my job. It's easy work, it'll be tough for a," coughs, "a fifth grader, but you'll be in a different grade by then. And you'll have that fat check I just cut. I was totally going to rip you off."

My body shrank to the size of a doll and I was shot into the diorama of the sky, where all bodies travel a flaming river into some great animal's eye.

Nada y Nada

charles thielman

Swaying on a downtown curb,
the dry gutters of his knuckles
wrapped around the neck of a bottle,
he's thin, tattered, unapproachable,
shouting at rush hour, opening
his evening's correspondence with madness
as shadows in combat etch walls,
snipers hissing in alleys.
Banned from buses, cafes, father
without photos, memory scattered
like dead robins beneath a skyscraper.

This driver prays: *Sleep, sleep, stifle the snapping whips*
of your veins
as neon stripes over the shut roads
in your eyes,
your combat-strung nerves needing veils
of soft blue calm.

Eyes like twin cougars brightened
by high-beams, his gaze arrows through
the monoxide wakes of the cubicle-released,
"Nada y Nada!"
Raising his arms, collecting mist bracelets
on stepladder wrists as he shouts
"Nada y Nada!"
Mind spun over the twisting switchbacks
of rotting bodies,
swaying on the curb, raising his arms,
perfecting his aim.

Sometimes I Hear Voices

stephen barber

The drought was in its second year. The coastal streams were dry, bedded in dust, and the grass parched and brittle. When my mother bathed my older brother and me she drew two inches of tepid water into the iron claw-foot tub and washed us together in the same bathwater. She rinsed our hair with watered vinegar and wrapped us in tattered towels to dry. Our younger brother was not at home. Our mother had sent him to live with her parents when the absence of our father became too burdensome.

One October morning after my mother had gone to work and my older brother had left with his friends, I locked the door, tossed the key under the mat, and scuffed along to Franklin School while dark clouds swept in off the Pacific Ocean. Large drops spattered against the street raising wisps of steam from the blacktop. Thunder ripped the clouds, tore them wide open, and the rain sheeted down, washing over pepper trees, eucalyptus, sycamores, and sent leaves and bits of paper at the side of the road rushing toward the storm drains. My white tee shirt, blue jeans, and high-top tennis shoes were soaked by the time I reached the shelter of the school buildings.

For seven days, dark clouds hung over the city, hid the mountains, while rain pelted down and turned the dry creek-beds into thrashing torrents that growled and clacked with the sound of tumbling rocks. Creekside trees washed out and tipped lazily into the rushing waters, releasing plumes of mud, and surged downstream. Sycamore Creek ran full. Eight years old, I stood on the bridge over the creek, and the floodwaters reached halfway to my knees.

Finally, the clouds thinned and the sun broke through. The rain stopped as suddenly as it had begun. The streams, muddy and surging in their banks, began to drop.

My mother took my brother and me to a Sunday morning service at the Gospel Tabernacle. The talk was about the drought, the rain, and God's benevolence. The sanctuary was full of words that drifted like butterflies. Dust motes sailed through the light that pooled along the stuccoed walls. The Reverend Hibble, raising his suited arms, thanked God for the answer to our prayers. The people sang hymns and the music flooded around our feet like zinnias and nasturtiums and trickled down the walls like bougainvillea.

Old Joe Moxcey, clothed in a brown suit that clung to his bony frame like some wrinkled castoff on a scarecrow, pulled himself up off his pew and, resting his hands on the back of the one in front of him, raised his old-man voice in thanks that his prayer for rain was answered. Then he added, for good measure, that he had to pray for the rain to stop so he could go outside and feed his rabbits. That prayer was answered too. Words like "thanks," "praise be," and "hallelujah" rustled in the space between the flowers and the shoes and the walls.

After old Joe Moxcey dropped back onto the pew, Leolia Watt stood and her words flowed out like more butterflies and some were fast like humming-birds, and they were all about her husband's sister, Doreen, but they flew by me because Joe Moxcey's rabbits were still in my head and I saw them resting in their cages and feeding on alfalfa pellets that old Joe Moxcey would have scattered.

Leolia Watt announced that her sister-in-law was certainly healed of her cancer. "She is feeling better," Leolia said, "and the doctors have been unable to find any remaining traces of the disease." She sat. The Hallelujahs came down like rose petals.

Cured of cancer. The power of prayer.

Grace Jackson, wearing a straw hat with a bouquet of plastic flowers on the brim, stood up and told us all how she had driven downtown and, unable to find a parking place, had asked God to intervene. Her prayer was answered when an old Mexican bracero in a battered Ford pickup pulled away from the curb, and there were more rose petals.

Reverend Hibble read from the bible. "If ye have faith as a grain of mus-tard seed, ye shall say unto this mountain, remove hence to yonder place; and it shall remove; and nothing shall be impossible unto you." Sunlight slanted down from the windows.

When he was through, we went home.

"Is that stuff true?" I asked.

"What stuff is that?"

"About moving mountains," I said.

"It's in the Bible," my mother said, "and that's the word of God."

What would you ask for if you could move a mountain?

The next day, after my mother and older brother were gone, I locked the door and hid the key under the mat again. I crossed the yard, squeezed through a thin spot in the Eugenia hedge, and walked up the street toward the school. I thought about old Joe Moxcey's rabbits. I wished I had a pet rabbit. My mother told me that my father had some rabbits when she met him. She said they were black and white. My father was gone now for almost four years; my little brother for two.

The idea that I could pray fastened on me as I walked by the corner where the old woman raised bird of paradise flowers, the ones my mother calls Strelitzia because my father was a gardener and he always called plants by their real names, she said. As I walked under a huge twisting live oak that shaded part of the street, the flowers spoke of my mother and father, and then there was the church service and Leolia Watt's sister-in-law and the rabbits and the grain of mustard seed.

That night, my mother tucked me in. She sat on the edge of my bed while I closed my eyes and said my prayers. She kissed me on the forehead, said goodnight, and pulled the door closed as she left. I waited until I was sure that she was gone before I threw off the covers, got out of bed, and knelt on the floor. I buried my face in the blankets and prayed.

"Please God bring my father home," I whispered into my blanket. "I have faith," I added.

When I was through, I crawled back into my bed, pulled the blanket up to my neck, and slipped into sleep as the prayer, like a honeybee, circled in my thoughts.

Sometimes I fell asleep kneeling by my bed and woke up later when the house was dark and quiet. I thought about how fine it would be when my father came home and everything would once more be the way it had been.

I dreamed that someone knocked on the door. When I opened it, my father was standing there. I didn't know whether to stay and hug him or to run and get my mother, but before I could move, the dream ended. I awakened and sat up in bed. I thought it was a sign. I prayed.

I didn't tell anyone about my plan, not even when my mother told me that she would take my brother and me to Camarillo to visit our father. I prayed every night until the day my mother finally loaded us in the Chevrolet and made the long drive to the state hospital. My brother rode shotgun in the front seat while I crawled into the space between the rear seat and the back window. I looked out at the passing landscape. When I thought of my father, I closed my eyes and prayed some more.

The doors were always locked at the hospital. My mother pushed a button that rang a bell inside the ward. We waited until a large man dressed in white with a cluster of keys hanging from his belt opened the door and let us in. We climbed stairs. At the top of the stairs was another door. The man with the keys unlocked it and ushered us into a large visiting room with steel tables and steel chairs painted dark green. The room was illuminated by high windows and made me think of dust and spiders and old men. It smelled like pee.

We sat down and waited while the man in white went to another door, unlocked it, went through and disappeared. Small groups of people sat at the tables and visited. They spoke in low voices, almost whispering. I heard the brass clack of the lock when the attendant returned and unlocked the door.

My father, dressed in blue jeans and a blue denim shirt, stepped through the door. The door slammed as he walked toward our table. There was something unusual about his clothing. Except for that, he looked like a man who could walk out of the hospital and go wherever he wanted.

I rushed to his side, threw my arms around his waist, and hugged him. His clothes were bulky and smelled like cigarette smoke. He put his arm over my shoulder and pulled me closer. My brother hugged him from the other side. Reluctantly, we turned him loose and all sat down.

"Why are you wearing so much clothing?" my mother asked.

"So much?" he asked. He unbuttoned his shirts. He wore four of them. He clearly wore more than one pair of jeans.

"Are you cold?" she asked. The room was not cold.

"Why would that matter?" he asked and shrugged. My mother didn't say more about his clothing.

Instead she reached under the table and brought up a brown paper grocery bag and set it in front of herself. "I brought you some things," she said. She reached into the bag and pulled out a carton of Lucky Strike cigarettes. She pushed it across the table to him. Next, she brought out a cellophane bag of hard candy and one of Spanish peanuts. She pushed them to the center of the table. He didn't reach for them.

"You shouldn't bring me these things," he said. He sat buttoning up his shirts.

"I know you like them." She pushed them closer to him.

"Don't you understand?" he said. "They'll just take them from me. Give them to the boys."

"Oh Charles," she said, "don't talk like that. Take them." She nudged them closer.

"Don't *Oh Charles* me," he said, his voice rising. "You don't know what this place is like. Nothing is good. Do you know what it is to have your every thought come wrapped in something you didn't think?" He stood up.

"Please," she said. She looked up at him. There were tears in the corners of her eyes.

"Have you seen the black people?" By this time, he was yelling. "They burn them here. That's why they're black. They're trying to do the same to me." The murmuring in the room stopped. When I turned around, everyone was looking at us.

"They're trying to help you," my mother said.

"Help me? How can you say that when you don't even know why I'm wearing all these clothes? Get me out of here before they kill me," he shouted.

"Please, Charles," she said, "the boys..."

A voice from the back of the room shrieked, "Oh ye of little faith..." and a balding, white haired man with glasses, sitting at a nearby table with an old woman and a young girl-child, sang out, "Oh God, please God, take me away from this place," and then he wept while the old woman put her arm over his shoulder and comforted him. The child edged away from him and closer to the old woman.

The man in white, the one with the keys, appeared. My mother nodded as he took my hand, my brother's hand, and led us to the door where we came in, unlocked it, led us out, locked it again, and walked us down the stairs. He left us confined in a courtyard where we sat on concrete steps and waited for our mother.

The futility of begging my mother to take my father home with us didn't deter me even as I knew she could only refuse. My father's madness, his dress and words, all locked him in that place. Prayer hadn't changed a thing. I finally had to accept the inevitable; my father was insane and would not come home. Love and silence were the only comfort I could give my mother. She had tears to shed, and mine only made hers the more bitter.

I couldn't tell anyone what I had done. The fault that kept my father in the hospital fell to me. I believed it was my lack of faith. That night, when my mother and brother had gone off to their beds and the darkness settled over my room, I pushed my face into my pillow and wept. The pillow was wet with my tears when the devil swept in on a breeze and whispered in my ear, "You could have saved him. You had only one thing to do, and that was to believe," he said.

"I believed," I said.

"Then why did you keep your plan a secret? As though I wouldn't know."

All this was long ago. First my father and then my mother died. And even now after all these years the devil comes to me, now an old man, and whispers in the night.

"You failed," he says, "and still you don't believe although you pretend otherwise. Why would you expect anything? You deserve nothing."

"Everyone knows the devil lies," I say, but there is no conviction in my voice.

Space Oddity (After Bowie)

tim raphael

(CNN)
Astronaut loses tool bag during spacewalk
Things didn't go quite according to plan for astronaut
Heide Stefanyshyn-Piper during her spacewalk
outside the International Space Station on Tuesday.

I'm the spacewalking astronaut
who let the tool bag float away
and watched it spin, black against black
across Orion's Belt. A split-
second is so quick up here. No
more than a peek at the shimmering
scars of cities sloughing the day.
Also, these gloves are a half-size too big.

Or I could be the solar panel
that began all this trouble. The crew
calls me balky, but what do they know
about life outside that Kevlar shell. Feed
me photons and I perform miracles
of power and light and urine recycling.
If I could rotate just a few degrees
everyone aboard could sleep.

More likely I'm the tool bag
orbiting ever closer to Earth. I
don't dread re-entry – my titanium
wrench knows the way. A star dust gift
from a meteor that long ago
made this same trip. I'll put on a show
for the herders when I blaze
across the Gobi sky.

But what if I'm the investigator
down at ground control in Houston?
Maybe I missed the cut
on the astronaut exam
and now spend my time
on fact finding missions.
My report would be a ballad
about the splendor in our mistakes.

Live Installation

e.g. willy

He imagined if someone or something reached out of the sky and ripped off his head, it wouldn't bother him. Not really. A decapitation at that moment might even be weirdly appropriate. He saw it already. The deed would be performed by the Shitarumpatouli, a rare bird he'd made up years earlier as a grad student, placed in all his paintings. It was a small icon, locked in a corner of the work, right above his signature, sometimes a caption by its beak, a pithy commentary on the *faits divers* of the universe, other times it was his expression or a turn of his bird body that reacted to the content of the paining. This morning it held a sword in its claws, was dribbling green and red ichor from its beak. He briefly watched his creature passing over the community center, wings flapping, descending. He ducked, wiped an arm over his face, and the Shitarumpatouli disappeared. It was replaced by a tree. He swore, stopped for a moment, steadied his shaking legs.

"Christ," he told himself, "you're no good. What are you even doing here? You should be at home, sleeping this off, not doing this. I mean, look at you. You're a wreck."

He continued walking, against his own advice.

As he passed the drive that led to the community center, he spied them. They were on the swings, waiting. Hillary, Dane, Matt, Silvia, and Riley. He managed a painful wave that shuddered through his body. They waved back.

"What the hell are you doing here? Get the hell out of here," he muttered, though he still kept heading up the hill towards the community center.

When he was close enough to be heard without raising his voice, he asked. "Hey guys, what's up?"

"Just waiting for the bus," Riley said. She was the leader of the eighth graders, the prettiest, already developed, attractive beyond her years, so she spoke first.

"Ah, very good," he croaked.

"It's late again," Matt said. He was swinging wildly as he said this, his feet some ten feet off the ground. Matt had on a little eye makeup, a touch of lipstick, a trench coat from Goodwill, the Pre-Goth look that middle schoolers flirted with.

He nodded. "Tell me something I don't know."

Riley said, "Oh, I don't know. Maybe some weird guy is talking to us in the park."

"Very funny," he said, grinning, though the grin was more like a dreadful, fatigued rictus. "Do you say that to everyone?"

"Just the pervs," Silvia injected.

He looked up the road to see if the bus was coming. The sun shone on his face, sent slicing shards of pain through his eyes. A shadow passed over his face. He smelled a strange, putrid odor. Was it his breath? Or was it the Shitarumpatouli returning? Christ, that would be appropriate. The forever mark of his career was rotting, a goddamned statement of his oeuvre to date. Now, instead of decapitation, it was residing in his mouth. He blinked, held a hand over his forehead, looked around. Nothing but traffic ahead on the entrance to the freeway, nearer by, a pack of women with strollers and infants, the Spring Valley bunch, mothers and nannies who met in the park every Friday morning, conversed with lattes in hand as they watched over their children.

He sat down on a bench by the swings, pushed himself into a position that would hold off collapse. They warily observed him as they swung back and forth. He sniffed, put a hand over mouth, checked his breath. Horrid. He reached into his pocket, found an old breath mint that he'd stashed there some time ago, popped it in his mouth. At least they weren't coming over. He had a few minutes to get himself together.

He considered, again, walking away. It would be the wisest thing to do. Staying up late with an old friend who was going to the Philippines in the morning for a sex reassignment operation—the full deal, penis removed, implants, hormones, injections, all for a very reasonable price that included a three week stay in a luxury hotel—had been a poor choice. These sorts of self-indulgences were best left for weekends and days off. Though, last night, it had appeared perfectly appropriate to pull an impromptu best buds skull-crusher dance party blowout on a weeknight because sex reassignment demanded that sort of thing. Steve was scared and excited. He needed a friend now that Steve was going to become Sheryl. That's what best buds do. They back each other up. Even midweek. Hence an evening of too many cocktails, exaggerated lungers of medical cannabis in the bathroom at the Top of the Mark, later the unfiltered cigarettes, the rails of cheap blow, dampened down with children's laxative, then dancing with a packed house of trannies at Divas. And after that? What was after that? Poor decisions. Bad calls. Shitty sleep. Shit. Fuck. Hell. Hungover, here, in the park, dressed in paint-stained clothes he'd picked off the floor of his rent-controlled apartment, hanging out with a pack of pubescent kids with attitude. This was not how you revived a career.

"Yeah, he does look especially pervy today," Matt said. He let his legs hang, slowed his trajectory. "Look at the face. Christ. I mean, shit."

He rubbed his unshaven beard. "Why are you guys always like this? Don't you ever give up?"

"Admit it, Martin, you love us," Riley said. "We're your favorites."

"Yeah, right."

They jumped off the swings, stood around him.

"You got any chocolate?" Riley demanded.

For a moment he saw nothing, just a white fog in front of him. He rubbed his face again and said, "What?"

"Last time you had chocolate," Riley said.

He shook his head, felt his brain sloshing from one side of the pan to the next. "No, I didn't."

"Yes, you did," Silvia said. "You had some of those bars from Trader Joe's."

"Oh, yeah, that's right," he said, vaguely remembering he'd shared a pack of chocolate bars with them as they waited for the bus.

"So, Martin, what do you have for us today?" Matt asked.

"No candy, I don't have anything," he said, though it came out more like a gasp, a telltale sign of his long night. "Sorry."

"Come on, you must have something," Hillary prodded. "Something in your bag."

"No, that's my lunch. I'm not sharing it with you."

Riley shifted her hip, struck a provocative pose. "Let's see what you brought."

On any other day he would have told them to get a damned clue. They could buy their own shitty lunch. Instead he shook his aching head, looked again up the road. The mothers and nannies were getting closer, lattes steaming. "There's nothing in that bag but a banana and a PBJ sandwich."

"I love PBJ's," Silvia said.

"I'm allergic to peanuts," Matt said. He reached into his trench coat, pulled out an inhaler, gave it a suck. He turned to Silvia. "Want a hit?"

"Naw, I got my own," she said.

He watched as the kids pulled out their inhalers, took deep blasts. He wondered if he could ask Matt for a hit, if that wouldn't be terribly inappropriate. No, it would be another poor decision. He should ride this out on his own power.

"Come on, show us the candy," Riley insisted, her eyes shining.

"Yeah, show us the candy like last time," Dane said, the quiet one with the ghostly eyes, hands crossed over her chest as if she were afraid.

"Show us the candy," Riley broadcasted as the mothers and nannies passed by. One mother glanced at him, a disgusted look on her face. Another had a cellphone, held it up in a defensive stance.

"Where's the candy?" Matt pled. "You promised candy."

A nanny gasped. The woman beside her pulled out her own phone, took a picture. He checked the road again. No bus. Fuck. Now he was a pervert. He pictured himself escaping, slipping down the hill like a frightened animal, the wounded Shitarumpatouli, a broken wing dragging, blood dripping from the tip, muttering excuses. This was why the galleries and the curators no longer called back. They had seen his failure way before he had noticed it himself. It was right in his paintings, erratic and self-indulgent. He had become his signature, the Shitarumpatouli, the bird monster. Not a painter any longer. Just a hungover old loser in the park. He couldn't even pay for studio space and now had to work in his kitchen with inferior paint, forced to beg for shows from tiny galleries, the "intimate" group shows, paintings placed at the back of the gallery by the bathroom. Pathetic. His production wobbling to a halt, the years of booze and self-medication, goddamned doing anything to keep his work out there.

The nannies and mothers finally moved on. He watched their heads together in exchange as they rolled up the hill towards the community center. One was tapping something into her phone.

"Come on, back to the swings. No candy here, guys," Riley said. "Just a dirty old man."

He remained on the bench, looked for the bus as the kids played. One of the mothers approached the group. He sighed, burped. Another blanket of white passed over his eyes, and he didn't notice the mother's whisper conversation with Riley until it was over and she was heading back up the hill.

"What did you say to that lady?" he asked, shifting uncomfortably on the bench. His arm moved on its own, a residual spasm of the phantom Shitarumpatouli emerging from his esophagus. He pushed himself backwards, clamped his arm between his body and the bench, burped a breath-mint burp.

"Nothing, just told her the pervy man in the filthy old jacket offered us candy the last time we saw him in the park," Riley said, smirking viciously. "And now we're kind of scared."

"Very funny. You didn't tell her that," he said.

"What do you think?" Riley asked.

He swallowed a gush of mucous and blood, the revenge for last night's cocaine indulgence, noticed his heart racing, the adrenalin juice of fear and dread.

"Yeah, yeah, she did," Matt said, laughing joyously. His lipstick was mostly gone now, just a line around the edges where the inhaler hadn't pulled it off.

"You're joking, right?"

"Joke? *Moi?*" Matt asked.

His stomach turned, and the night of bad decisions came rolling up through his guts into his throat. He gulped, winced, wiped his mouth. He should have been prepared for this, seen this coming. He knew them all, the postmodern progeny shitbirds of the Shitarumpatouli, their histories at the Bradford Academy. Matt, the kid who'd called in the bomb scare, got the whole school swept with bomb-sniffing dogs just so he wouldn't have to do his Social Studies project. Riley, whose father was a tech startup mogul for an online dating app, and who was openly dating a senior boy in the dorms. Hillary, the girl who'd been featured in a Rolling Stone article for the children of the rich and neglected. Dane, the quiet one, who wrote dark, scary prose on all her English assignments. Silvia, the niece of a Salvadoran oligarch, very sweet until you assigned her anything less than an A, and then the phone calls started with thinly veiled threats. So why was he so foolish that it had to get to this? Or perhaps it did have to go this far for him to see. This was the course of his story, the stamp of the Shitarumpatouli. It had always been the course, the chaos in all of his paintings. This fuckswamp hangover day.

Hillary said, "You should've seen her face, it was epic."

"Yeah, epic," Dane agreed.

"You didn't tell them that I'm your art teacher?" he asked, his voice slippery with snot and saliva. "You didn't point out that you go to a very exclusive private school? That we're waiting for the bus to pick us up and take us to the MOMA for a day of one-on-one instruction with Manuel Neri?"

"Naw, we thought we'd mess with you instead," Riley said and followed it with a sharp titter.

He snorted, swallowed the streaming glob of mucous, coughed as some went the wrong direction. "Jesus Christ. You don't pull that on people. Ever. It's not funny."

"Sure it is," Matt said, a grin plastered on his face. "We so got you."

"Come on, you're joking, right?" He checked again.

"Joke? We never joke," Silvia said flatly, her voice cool like her death-squad uncle's when her grades went down.

Riley said, "Never."

He spat out a wad of bloody snot on the pavement. "Fuck," he said. He looked up the hill at the Spring Valley nanny-mother coalition. He knew without seeing their screens that every last one was on the phone, autodialing the police, uploading pictures of the pervy man to their nextdoor.com account. Fuck. Shit. Fuck. Shit. Fuck. Any minute a cop car was going to pull up, followed by the bus, and thirty kids would witness the weirdo in the park getting tackled, then cuffed. He deserved this. It was his own doing. The new generation of art buyers were tech kids who wanted Pokémon statues in their million-dollar lofts. No one gave a shit about real paint on canvas, real emotions, real life depictions. He had done what all exhibiting artists do when sales are down, he'd taken a job teaching at-risk rich kids. A goddamned cliché.

"Fuck," he said again.

"You got that?" Riley asked, holding up her phone.

"Yeah," Matt said. "Every frame. Pervy teacher spitting blood, using vulgarity around impressionable middle-schoolers. Classic."

Silvia flashed her phone. "Me too. My uncle's gonna love it."

"Hope you're ready for this ride, Martin," Dane said, her ghostly eyes shining like nickel moons.

His guts did another nauseating roll. He blinked, saw the third curtain of white pass over his sight, felt the blood leave his face, the Shitarumpatouli flying in a metaphysical death curve back into his body. "Oh, Christ, no," he groaned.

Matt said, "Dude, look at your face."

He broke into a furious run towards the community center bathroom. It was the broken-winged Shitarumpatouli run, the crab-like scuttle, the icon of decay and desperation.

"You should've brought those chocolates," Riley admonished as he fled.

Although he prayed he was going to make it to the open door, he knew he was going to vomit on the manicured lawn. A messy way to end his teaching career, the Bradford Academy way. He'd seen it happen to teachers just like him. The kids were experts at finding weaknesses, then exploiting them. The list of educators that had passed through the Bradford Academy was embarrassingly long. Christ. This was his job-ender moment. They'd been waiting for him to blow it, had timed it perfectly. And he'd walked straight into it. He still prayed, hoped, scrambled, as if it made some kind of difference, as if he really thought he was going to get through the wicked ritual.

He fell, as he had predicted. His hands landed on the lawn. He realized quite suddenly that it was a harder landing than expected. The jolt was tremendous. A fart busted loose from his trembling haunches. It tooted a ghastly, wailing note.

They laughed in unison at his failure.

Matt extended his phone in front of him like a shield. "This is so going on Facebook."

"Snapchat," Riley said. She stretched out the vowels of the word, then closed them shut with the stinging T-consonant that made the word sound horrifying.

Dane's face shined wickedly as she watched the road. "Hey, guys, I think I see the police."

Riley began to make frantic gestures to the approaching vehicle. "Help! Help!" she shouted.

"Here comes the bus too," Matt said. "Epic."

Hillary said, "Dude, this is the best field trip ever."

"Lit," Silvia agreed.

Riley nodded. "So lit."

He resisted the building pressure from his torso, but then threw up a fresh gush of sweet vomit. It was a Shitarumpatouli puke, viscous and brightly hued. Out came the undigested cherries from last night's Manhattans, the pieces of shrimp étouffée that were his late-night attempt to get sober snack. He tried to steady himself, felt his arms collapsing. He landed face-first in his bile, pushed himself up, slipped again. He heard the doors of the police car opening, Riley shouting, then the voices of authority: "On the ground! Stay on the ground!"

He pressed his face into the grass, eyes closed, and saw through the back of his skull the Shitarumpatouli circling overhead, dark wings flapping, talons prepared to rip off his head. He futilely wished that YouTube "Teacher Gone Bad" videos weren't really as popular as they used to be. Even with his face covered in vomit, he wished he were anywhere but here. A decapitation right now would be appropriate, a real escape route.

"Agh, agh," he gargled.

Briefly after he'd thrown up, his mind felt clear and sharp, and he could see the outcome, his ghastly end. It was as it had been painted. The Shitarumpatouli's naked toll. The poignant comments of a strange bird-thing would at last come to roost, became text at the bottom of the YouTube video, an imbedded explanation of his horror. This was how it was meant to end. Teacher Gone Bad.

No, no, no, no. He rose, scrambled again towards the bathroom.

"On the ground!" the police repeated in unison.

"No, not this, no way," he growled, arms flailing.

Matt explained, "Oh, hell yeah."

"On the ground sir!"

"Fuck no!" he said. "Hell fucking no!"

"On the ground, sir!"

He spun, faced their cellphones. He was wrenched by another convulsion. "I'm not a threat!" He tried to modulate his voice, keep it comprehensible, but it came out as a pitchy squawk, the true voice of the Shitarumpatouli.

Two of the police officers had their TASER X2 Defender's drawn. A third stood at a distance with a Beretta 92 pistol.

The officer with the gun ordered, "On the ground."

"Don't shoot! Don't shoot!" he squawked again.

The laser-guided, semi-automatic taser struck his thorax. He danced and twisted, puked and pissed.

"Stop! Stop!" he cried, then fell to his knees, his body torquing. He turned, stood up halfway, kicked, spewed.

"On the ground!" reiterated the cop with the gun.

"I'm an artist! An artist!" he declared as the next taser blast rippled through his body, sending him into cardiac arrest. The police descended and the blows began. He fought to get his face to the cellphone cameras. He stuck his tongue out, grimaced, bit a cop. The cop smashed a fist into his head, and he puked again to where he thought the cameras would be. There was no going back. Not now. Not goddamned ever.

"Stop! No!" A piercing pain sliced through his heart. He grinned crazily when he saw the bus turning into the parking lot. Every window was open, hands reaching out, phones turned towards him. Oh, those beautiful hands, waving like the feet of a centipede. He pulled his lips above his gums, coughed, gagged. His bowels rumbled, evacuated. His ears rang. His skin burned. His body shook with uncontrolled fits. He felt bizarrely uplifted, happy even. A strange voice gurgled in his ear, and he realized it was his own, that he was giggling. Yes, yes, yes. Perfect. He was back on his game. Christ. Wonderful. The Shitarumpatouli was rising again at last. Yes, sweet, goddamned, yes. Just what his career needed and the art world demanded, a lovely, tortured ending, videos jumping from one device to the next. Viral shit. Man dying. God, the relief. No more dumpster diving because his paycheck went to rent, booze, and horribly expensive art supplies. No more entitled rich kids. No more begging for one-man shows in a cruel, heartless market. This wasn't a decapitation, or a lopped off ear, it was so much better.

Ricky the Racoon

hannah stahle metcalf

Ricky the Raccoon ate like a king. Watermelon rinds, gnawed up rib bones, apple cores. Anything that would have stunk up the trash or could be considered vaguely biodegradable came sailing over the railing of the back porch with sporadic frequency. On nights that the extended family gathered and feasted at my grandparents' house, so did Ricky the Raccoon. And in late summer, when the Midwest corn was at its sweetest, juicy corn-cobs rained down on Ricky the Raccoon like manna from heaven.

For as long as I knew them my grandparents didn't own a pet, but they named the raccoon that hung around their house on Lake Michigan. My mom remembers a book from her childhood where a family took in a raccoon and named him Racky. Perhaps my grandparents found the story endearing and adopted it into their lives. Or perhaps they had heard the Beatles' song, "Rocky Raccoon," one too many times and wanted to associate raccoons again with childhood wonder instead of revenge-murder in a dank saloon. Whatever the reason, they named that little night prowler Ricky, started feeding him their table scraps, and never looked back.

Forest floor turned corn graveyard as cob after cob landed in a near silent rustle-thud where the tree line ran along the perimeter of the porch. In my family, corn throwing felt like a rite of passage. While Ricky was thought on with fondness, my grandparents preferred the raccoon to keep his distance from the house. You were only allowed to throw a corncob if you could get it far enough away to ensure Ricky kept his distance. It was a display of strength that I was incapable of, due to lank and an alarming lack of coor-dination, until I was close to pre-teen. For years I reluctantly handed my corncob off to an uncle or older cousin, wary that my skinny arms wouldn't be able to send the corncob far enough from the house. I watched in strange envy as the rest of my family members cradled the cobs loosely in their hands, cocked their elbows, and called out, "Here Ricky, Ricky!"

As a child, I thought of our discarded corncobs as gifts bestowed on the grateful forest creature. It was every little girl's dream: communing with nature and building a relationship with tiny furry creatures. I fancied myself an aspiring Cinderella or Snow White. Soon, I imagined, Ricky would be helping me clean up my room and reading me bedtime stories.

My infatuation with Ricky went beyond daydreams of myself as a Disney princess though. As a little girl from Alaska, the fact that the creature I communed with was a raccoon added another layer of whimsy. Growing up in the land of perpetual summertime-light meant no stargazing, no light-ning bugs, and an environment that could not support the nocturnal life of raccoons.

Ricky was exotic, not just for the way my family anthropomorphized him, but because he represented a part of the world that didn't exist in my life in Alaska. Where some kids might be fascinated by an illuminated night, I was positively bored. I wanted the darkness and the things that came with it. My idea of exotic was admittedly warped, but it was the lens through which I viewed the world and, in some ways, still do. I always notice when the stars are out, especially if it's warm enough outside to watch them wink without shivering myself.

An adult with perspective will realize that the rest of my family did not share the same relationship with Ricky that I harbored. One might wonder how my grandparents could nurture a certain level of affection for the raccoon—enough affection to name it—while also adamantly maintaining that the corncobs be thrown *far*. A distance with the purpose of ensuring Ricky not get too attached or associate the food too closely with the house.

As an adult, I came to the upsetting realization that I never actually laid eyes on Ricky. Perhaps my grandparents' insistence about the corncobs had been successful and Ricky never had any reason to go rummaging through the garbage or scurrying around the garden. In fact, the only time I saw a raccoon at the house at all was one late night when a lady raccoon and a few of her kits came scratching at the back-screen door. Since it was a lady raccoon, I assumed it wasn't Ricky. Still, my brother and I sat in awe at the sight of an actual raccoon. We pressed our hands against the glass with the same wonder that Tarzan must have had upon meeting Jane, and snapped pictures with my mom's digital camera. The raccoons didn't seem bothered by the popping light of the flash. I don't remember if my grandparents were bothered by the raccoon's proximity to the house.

As summers passed and I began to understand the realistic lifespans of animals compared to humans, I recognized that Ricky was more family folklore than real raccoon. Since Ricky's origin story began around the time my grandparents started building the house in 1967, he would have had to have been well into his tenth raccoon life by the time my adult relatives began to pass down that particular aspect of our family's oral tradition to me.

I heard once that the light from the nearest star takes four years to reach Earth. By the time the light is made real for us here, it is already a distant memory for the star. And that's just the nearest star. The light from the farthest star from Earth was discovered on April 9, 2009. I say the *light* was discovered, because the star is 112,900,000,000 light years away from Earth, and so it seems the most impossible thing for us to ever discover the star itself—that unreachable source of light.

I'm not sure exactly when the tale of Ricky the Raccoon began, but I am familiar with the iterations and memories of Ricky that have reached me.

My grandparents sold their house more than ten years ago, and still I think of Ricky whenever I bite into a corncob and lodge a kernel in the tight space between my teeth. I am the last generation that Ricky the Raccoon has made memories with.

Stars are just memories that come out every night. Altogether undeterred by our ability to see them, unbothered that clouds, or proximity to the sun might obscure them, or discouraged that by the time their light travels that impossible distance down to Earth, there is a slim chance that anyone might stop to look at them. Who's to say that the impossibility of Ricky the Raccoon is any less real than a star's, or that his memory might go on reaching?

Three Fortune Cookies

carla ann mcgill

Tomorrow the Seas of Your Life Will be Calm
    Are the seas within or without? The outside can be calm, the palm trees on either side of the street looking superbly serene in the angled light, while the inside can be disrupted. Volcanic. Collapsing. Florida, all our golden light saturating the shorelines, the golf courses, the paved curves at Disney World. Here at the high school in the aftermath, though the shadows by the road dance in the dappled light of nearby foliage, yes things are calm, and were even quiet for a few moments after it was done. The cars move by like fish in the sea, and they are calmly disturbed and violently still. This is the calm after the ferocity, after the outburst, after the fall of the seventeen. I was only a mother for three months, but I am feeling the pain of the other mothers today. I read something once about how no one knows another's anguish, not completely. We are all alone in some philosophical way. Here there will be the sounds of keys and doors. I am driving slowly by, but even I can hear the screams, as I head back to my house by the sea. The sea, often calm, and then abruptly the waves rise up like hot lava, like leviathans from an ancient sacred text.

A Pleasant Surprise is in Store for You
    I suppose from a certain perspective. My son was alive, after all. I didn't fall apart, at least not visually, not verbally. I held on to the silent place inside, ignoring the noise around it, all the terrible possibilities. I held on because I had recently had a temper tantrum over something silly, something insignificant. Now I felt myself go to the opposite interior terrain. The place of silence. The place of dread. The place of appalling possibilities. But a place of quiet. It is hard to be human. To know that we will die at all, at any time in our future, and to deal with the realities of the body in space and in time. It is nearly intolerable to realize that we all face the ultimate loss and in thousands of imaginable ways. Yet as I drove to the school to be with the other parents, and I saw the police cars and the students running out, I found myself noticing the almost perfect weather, a little warm, mildly humid. Though I am a father, a man who has been at war for our nation, I felt the impulse to fall into the arms of the officer, to beg him to explain the world to me. Instead, I looked for my boy, and there he was, running to me. He ran into my arms, crying as he did when he was four or five years old. The sunlight seemed to open my chest and flow inside as I held him, and all the world seemed to spin and dance and grieve and groan. The days since have been cold, even though the weather is warm. They have been cold and dry, and as I look out over the suburbs, I hear the snarl of lions, the cruel

whistle of snowy winds, and the faster, sharp barrage of gunfire. I am still at odds with the givens, our life-headed-to-death, the terrible realities we are born into. Tomorrow, even so, we will attend Mass and we will observe the Lenten season. The observations and meditations on our lives here in this strange and aching place and beyond in a place we imagine and into which we pour our hope.

You Will Soon be the Center of Attention

The comedian had waited a long time before he went back to doing stand-up. How could he make comedy out of divorce?

The room was about half-full at the Last Laughs Comedy Club in Parkland, Florida, which was somewhat surprising after last week's high school massacre. The audience looked typical, as he could see from his peek through the black curtain from the side of the stage. Most of them looked like thirty-somethings, with a few AARP folks in the crowd too, all middle-class, as far as he could tell.

He used to perform here at least once a month, but that was before he found out about his wife's betrayal. Laughter, applause. He was up.

Applause. Silence. A few warm up comments. Then his routine.

"So, I'm divorced now." Sounds from the audience, "ahs" and "ohs."

"Yeah, I had what they call a photo bomb marriage. There was another guy in the picture."*

A couple of loud laughs, some chuckles.

He was surprised that anyone felt like laughing, but perhaps it was the proverbial tonic for recent traumas. He thought of the shooter, the sudden notoriety. Fame could come for many reasons, he knew, and attention could be good or bad.

"So, I'm dating a woman now. Well, she's a stripper. I took her out to dinner at this one place I like. And I got what I always get: an erection."*

More chuckles.

"But you know, I felt kind of sorry for her. I was looking at her, and I thought, gee, she's gone about as low as a person can go in society. She's now dating a comedian."*

Good, hearty laughs. He wondered if he should mention the school shooting. Is it better to include it or ignore it? Should he tell them about the friend he lost to a different shooter some years ago? Somehow, he couldn't bring himself to come up with any jokes about shootings, or guns, or insanity.

He had been reading the papers all morning, looking at the anguished faces of the families of dead teens. The face of the shooter. Attention can be overrated.

---

*Comedic standup routine material used with permission from Jim Barnes @ jimbarnescomedy.com

Issue 8 Contributors

Devon Balwit lives scarily close to the Cascadia Subduction Zone. Her individual poems can be found or are forthcoming in a host of anthologies and in journals such as *The Cincinnati Review, apt, Posit, Grist, The Aeolian Harp Folio, Triggerfish, Fifth Wednesday, The Free State Review, The Carolina Quarterly, Rattle*, etc. For more about her chapbooks and her collections, see her website at: https://pelapdx.wixsite.com/devonbalwitpoet

Stephen Barber is an old guy living in Portland, Oregon where he writes, does a little woodworking, and hikes in the Gorge with his dog. He graduated from UCSB with a BA in literature.

Cathleen Calbert's writing has appeared in many publications, including *Ms. Magazine, The New Republic, The New York Times*, and *The Paris Review*. She is the author of four books of poetry: *Lessons in Space, Bad Judgment, Sleeping with a Famous Poet*, and *The Afflicted Girls*. Her awards include The Nation Discovery Award, a Pushcart Prize, the Sheila Motton Book Prize, and the Vernice Quebodeaux Poetry Prize for Women.

Lorraine Hanlon Comanor was a U.S. figure skating champion and world team member. She received a B.A. from Harvard University, a M.D. from Stanford University School of Medicine, and a M.F.A. from The Bennington Writing Seminars. A board-certified anesthesiologist and pharmaceutical consultant, she has co-authored 36 medical publications. She has also been a Pushcart nominee. Mother of three, and grandmother of one, she is an avid hiker and lives in Truckee and Carmel Valley.

Peter Clarke is the author of the comic novel "Politicians Are Superheroes" (Pski's Porch Publishing, 2018). His short fiction has appeared in publications including *3AM Magazine, Curbside Splendor*, and *Hobart*. He's the founding editor of *Jokes Literary Review*. Native to Port Angeles, Washington, he currently lives in Oakland, California. See: www.petermclarke.com.

Gabe Congdon lives in Seattle where he is one of the creators of the web-series &@. He has two cats. One is Touch Focus and the other is Weegee.

Beau Ewan is an English professor at the University of Hawaii's Kapiolani Community College. His writing has appeared in the *The Chronicle of Higher Education, Hawaii Pacific Review, Honolulu Civil Beat, The Macguffin, Poydras Review*, and several surfing magazines: *Surfing, Surfer, The Surfer's Path, Eastern*

Surf Magazine, and *Tracks*. When he is not teaching, writing, or surfing, he is out hiking with his beautiful wife, Nathalie, and his ill-behaved rescue dog, Nala.

Linda Ferguson is an award-winning writer of poetry, fiction and essays. Her poetry chapbook was published by Dancing Girl Press. She has a passion for teaching creative writing classes that inspire and support students of all ages. https://bylindaferguson.blogspot.com/

Gabriela Denise Frank is a literary artist working across fiction, nonfiction, poetry and performance. Her writing has appeared in *True Story*, *Crab Creek Review*, *Lunch Ticket*, *The Rumpus*, *Front Porch Journal* and the blogs of *Brevity* and *Submittable*. A native of Detroit, Michigan, she now calls the Pacific Northwest home. www.gabrieladenisefrank.com

Stephanie Barbé Hammer has published short stories, poems and lyric essays in *GRAVEL*, *Birds We Piled Loosely*, *Pearl*, and the *Hayden's Ferry Review* among other places. She is the author of the novel, *The Puppet Turners of Narrow Interior*, the poetry collection *How Formal?* and a how-to-write magical realism manual, *Delicious Strangeness*. A Manhattanite, and then a Los Angeles resident, Stephanie lives, writes and kvetches about the paucity of dry cleaners in rural Washington State.

Michele N. Harmeling is a poet and essayist residing in picturesque Palmer, Alaska. Her work has appeared in such publications as the *Alaska Quarterly Review*, *Juked Magazine*, *Reed Magazine*, and the *Adirondack Review*; she is the recipient of the 2009 Whiskey Island Poetry Prize. Her spare time is generally spent foraging for wild edibles, backpacking, fishing, reading and lavishing attention on her son Walker, and dog Puck.

Myrlin A. Hermes is the author of the novels *Careful What You Wish For* and the Lambda award-winning *The Lunatic, the Lover, and the Poet*, called "witty, erudite, and decidedly sexy" by Booklist. Her poetry has appeared in Sheela-Na-Gig and the Notre Dame Review. A graduate of Reed College and the University of London, she lives in Portland, Oregon, where she finds an unusual number of four-leaf clovers.

Deanna Hershiser lives in Eugene, Oregon with her husband and an elderly orange cat. Her writing has been published or is forthcoming in *Rosebud*, *Palooka Magazine*, *Runner's World*, and elsewhere. She works in a bookstore, blogs at https://storieshappen.blogspot.com, and wanders beside the Willamette River, ever anticipating visits from her grandson.

In a past century, Heikki Huotari attended a one-room school and spent summers on a forest-fire lookout tower. He is now a retired math professor and has published three chapbooks, one of which won the Gambling The Aisle prize, and one collection, *Fractal Idyll* (A..P Press). Another collection is in press.

Chad W. Lutz was born in Akron, Ohio, in 1986 and raised in the neighboring suburb of Stow. Alumna of Kent State University's English program, Chad earned an MFA in Creative Writing at Mills College and currently serves as an associate editor for Pretty Owl Poetry. His writing has been featured in *KYSO Flash, Foliate Oak Literary Magazine, Haunted Waters Press*, and was awarded the 2017 prize in literary fiction by Bacopa Review. Chad took second overall at the 2016 Two Cities Marathon in Fresno, CA, and has competed in five Boston Marathons.

Hannah Stahle Metcalf was born and raised in Wasilla, Alaska, but left her home state to pursue a degree in English Literature at the University of North Carolina Wilmington. She currently resides in Spokane, Washington, where she is pursuing her MFA in Creative Nonfiction from Eastern Washington University. When she's not waiting for the next season of The Great British Baking Show to come out on Netflix, Hannah enjoys spending time outside with her husband.

Carla Ann McGill earned her doctorate in English from the University of California, Riverside. Her work has been published in *A Clean Well-Lighted Place, The Atlanta Review, Shark Reef, Crack the Spine, Westview, Common Ground Review, Caveat Lector, Inland Empire Magazine, Vending Machine Press, Schuylkill Valley Journal of the Arts, Streetlight Magazine, The Penmen Review, Cloudbank, Burningword, The Alembic, Broad River Review, Paragon Journal*, and *Poets' Espresso Review*. Her story, "Thirteen Memories," received an Honorable Mention in Glimmer Train's MAR/APR 2016 Very Short Fiction Contest. She lives in Rancho Cucamonga, CA with her husband, and writes poetry and fiction.

José Enrique Medina earned his BA in English from Cornell University. He writes poems, short stories and novels. His work has appeared in *The Burnside Review, Reed Magazine, American Writers Review*, and other publications. When he is not writing, he enjoys playing with his baby chicks, bunnies and piglets on his farm in Whittier, California.

Chris Menezes has a BA in Creative Writing from CSU Long Beach and an MFA in poetry from Converse College. His work has appeared in *Switchback, RipRap, Pearl Magazine, Buck Off Magazine, Foliate Oak*, and Z-Publishing's *Best Emerging Poets of California*. In addition to working as a freelance writer and substitute teacher in Riverside, California, he reads poetry submissions for *Carve Magazine* and *South 85 Journal*.

Besides short stories, JoAnneh Nagler has published three nonfiction books: *Naked Marriage*; *How to Be an Artist*; and *The Debt-Free Spending Plan*, two of which were Amazon Top-100 books. She authored the new play *Ruby and George in Love* (Sonoma Arts Live Theatre Company, 2018), and has written music and lyrics for two music CD's, *I Burn* and *Enraptured*. Find these and more at www.AnArtistryLife.com

David JS Pickering's poetry has been published in the *Raven Chronicles, Sunday Oregonian, Portland Review, Gertrude Journal*, in the anthology *Salt*, and online at *NonBinary Review*. He earns his living as a Human Resource Director and he makes time on Saturdays to write in the best coffee shop he can find. David recently moved from Portland with his husband to The Dalles, a town sadly bereft of good coffee joints. He continues to write, anyway.

Tim Raphael lives with his family in the Mt. Tabor neighborhood of Portland, Oregon. His poems have appeared in *Windfall, Cirque, The Timberline Review, Canary, Verseweavers* and *Moments Before Midnight*, a 2018 anthology of Oregon poets. He was a 2017 prize winner in the Oregon Poetry Association's New Poet's category.

Tanyo Ravicz grew up in Los Angeles, graduated from Harvard University, and settled in Alaska, where he worked in a variety of fields. He moved back to California, and in the summers he returns to his Kodiak Island homestead. His book *Alaskans* is a collection of his short stories, and his novel *A Man of His Village* relate the odyssey of a migrant farm worker from Mexico to Alaska.

Ron Riekki's books include A*nd Here: 100 Years of Upper Peninsula Writing, 1917-2017* (Michigan State University Press), *Here: Women Writing on Michigan's Upper Peninsula* (Michigan State University Press, 2016 Independent Publisher Book Award Gold Medal Great Lakes Best Regional Fiction), *The Way North: Collected Upper Peninsula New Works* (Wayne State University Press, 2014 Michigan Notable Book awarded by the Library of Michigan), and *U.P.: a novel* (Ghost Road Press).

Katherine Robbins is originally from California and currently works in Tokyo as an international preschool teacher. She writes both fiction novels and predominantly free verse poetry. Her poems have been published by *Dragon Poet Review*. She also specializes in photography, some of which has been published by various magazines and sites including *Sleeklens, Expert Photography*, and *Transcendence Magazine*.

Kaylie Saidin grew up in the San Francisco Bay area and now lives in New Orleans. She is an assistant fiction editor at *Pithead Chapel*, an editor at the *Loyola Maroon*, and a former intern editor at the *New Orleans Review*. She won the 2018 Dawson Gaillard Award for Fiction and has been nominated for the Best of the Net Anthology. You can read more of her in *Jellyfish Review, Every Pigeon, Porridge Magazine*, and other journals at kayliesaidin. weebly.com.

Anthony Seidman is a poet translator from Los Angeles. His translations have appeared in journals like *World Literature Today, Latin American Literature Today, Huizache, Nimrod*, and *Modern Poetry In Translation*. His own poems are published regularly in such journals as *The Bitter Oleander, Poetry Inter-*

national, *Black Herald*, *Ambit*. Other work has been included in anthologies like *The Ecopoetry Anthology* (Trinity University Press). His most recent books include *A Sleepless Man Sits Up In Bed* (Eyewear Publishing, London), *Crows: Translations from Roberto Castillo Udiarte* (Business Bear Press, Los Angeles), and *Confetti-Ash: Selected Poems of Salvador Novo* (The Bitter Oleander Press, New York).

John Sperry is a writer and printmaker from Sonoma. His work has previously appeared in *Ambit*, *Grub Street*, and the *New Lit Salon*.

Charles Thielman was raised in Charleston, S.C., and Chicago. He was educated at red-bricked universities and on city streets. He has enjoyed working as a social worker, truck driver, city bus driver, and enthused bookstore clerk. He is a grandfather, poet, artist, and president of a county-wide writer's organization, Lane Literary Guild. A video of his reading at Tsunami Books, Eugene, OR—http://www.youtube.com/watch?v=d-5-G_jaoJY

Derek Updegraff is the author of the fiction collection T*he Butcher's Tale and Other Stories* (2016) and the poetry collection *Paintings That Look Like Things* (2018), both from Stephen F. Austin State University Press. His short stories, poems, and translations have appeared in *The Carolina Quarterly*, *CutBank*, *The Greensboro Review*, *Hobart*, *the minnesota review*, *North Dakota Quarterly*, *The Southampton Review*, and other places. He is an associate professor of English at Azusa Pacific University.

Katherine Van Eddy is a California-born poet living in Tacoma, Washington. She earned a BA in Creative Writing and MAT in Elementary Education from the University of Puget Sound. Her poems have appeared in *Crosscurrents* (University of Puget Sound), *Creative Colloquy Volume 4*, and *HoosierLit*. She currently teaches 3rd/4th grade at a Catholic school while moonlighting as a writer and runner.

Charlotte Van Werven recently graduated from Corban University with a bachelor's degree in creative writing. She writes because art demands thought, and the act of writing teaches her about herself and others. She wrote "Gethsemane for Beginners" as a way to process the adoption of her brother and to try to understand a little more about him and his place in her family. Her work has also appeared in *Into the Void*.

E.G. Willy is a Northern California writer. His short stories in English have appeared in *Conjunctions*, *Zyzzyva*, *J Journal*, *The Berkeley Review*, and the *Redwood Coast Review*. Anthologies that have included his writings are *Stories From Where We Live*, *Milkweed Editions*, *The Breast*, *Global City Press*, *Creatures of Habitat*, *Mint Hill Books*, and *Lock and Load*, a Second Amendment Reader from the University of New Mexico Press. Willy is something of a loner. He lives in a nowhere town that has a public library, a police station, a fire station, a shopping district, a few schools, and not a single bookstore.